The Complete Thai Dessert Cookbook

The Best Dessert Recipes, Straight Out of Thailand!

Urassaya Manaying

TABLE OF CONTENTS

Introduction 1

Thai Cooking Basics 3
Basic Cooking Methods 4
Handy Tools for Thai Cooking 6

Basic Food Substitutions 7

Dipping Sauces, Salsas, and Vinaigrettes 9
- 5-Minute Dipping Sauce 9
- Banana, Tamarind, and Mint Salsa 9
- Ginger-Lemongrass Vinaigrette 10
- Jalapeño-Lime Vinaigrette 10
- Mango-Cucumber Salsa 11
- Mango-Pineapple Salsa 11
- Mint-Cilantro "Chutney" 12
- Minty Dipping Sauce 12
- Peanut Dipping Sauce — 1 13
- Peanut Dipping Sauce — 2 13
- Peanut Dipping Sauce — 3 14
- Peanut Pesto 15
- Quick Hot Dipping Sauce 15
- Spicy Thai Dressing 16
- Sweet-and-Sour Dipping Sauce 16
- Thai-Style Plum Dipping Sauce 17

Thai Curry Pastes, Marinades, and Other Concoctions 18
- Asian Marinade — 1 18
- Asian Marinade — 2 18
- Black Bean Paste 19
- Chili Tamarind Paste 20
- Chili Vinegar 21
- Coconut Marinade 21
- Green Curry Paste — 1 22
- Green Curry Paste — 2 23
- Lemon Chili Vinegar 23
- Lemongrass Marinade 24
- Malaysian Marinade 24
- Minty Tamarind Paste 25
- Northern (or Jungle) Curry Paste 25
- Red Curry Paste — 1 26
- Red Curry Paste — 2 27
- Shredded Fresh Coconut 28
- Southern (or Massaman) Curry Paste 28
- Tamarind Concentrate 29
- Tamarind Marinade 30
- Thai Grilling Rub 30
- Thai Marinade — 1 31
- Thai Marinade — 2 31
- Thai Marinade — 3 32

Thai Vinegar Marinade	33
Yellow Bean Sauce	33

Desserts — 35

Banana Coconut Soup	35
Bananas Poached in Coconut Milk	35
Citrus Fool	36
Coconut Custard	37
Coconut-Pineapple Soufflé for 2	37
Crispy Crepes with Fresh Fruit	38
Fresh Oranges in Rose Water	39
Lemongrass Custard	40
Mango Fool	41
Mango Sauce over Ice Cream	41
Pineapple Rice	42
Pineapple-Mango Sherbet	43
Pumpkin Custard	43
Pumpkin Simmered in Coconut Milk	44
Steamed Coconut Cakes	44
Sticky Rice with Coconut Cream Sauce	45
Sweet Sticky Rice	46
Taro Balls Poached in Coconut Milk	46
Tofu with Sweet Ginger	47
Tropical Coconut Rice	48
Tropical Fruit with Ginger Creème Anglaise	48
Watermelon Ice	49

Appetizers — 51

3-Flavor Rice Sticks	51
Basil and Shrimp Wedges	51
Chicken, Shrimp, and Beef Satay	52
Chinese-Style Dumplings	53
Cold Sesame Noodles	54
Crab Spring Rolls	55
Crispy Mussel Pancakes	56
Curried Fish Cakes	57
Fried Tofu with Dipping Sauces	58
Fried Won Tons	58
Mee Krob	59
Omelet "Egg Rolls"	60
Pork Toast Triangles	62
Pork, Carrot, and Celery Spring Rolls	63
Rice Paper Rolls	64
Salt-Cured Eggs	64
Shrimp Toast	65
Skewered Thai Pork	66
Son-in-Law Eggs	67
Spicy Coconut Bundles	67
Spicy Ground Pork in Basil Leaves	68
Spicy Scallops	69
Thai Fries	70

Soups — 72

Asian Chicken Noodle Soup _____ 72
Chicken Soup with Lemongrass _____ 73
Chilled Mango Soup _____ 74
Lemony Chicken Soup _____ 74
Pumpkin Soup _____ 75
Spicy Seafood Soup _____ 77
Thai-Spiced Beef Soup with Rice Noodles _____ 78
Tom Ka Kai _____ 79
Tom Yum _____ 79
Vegetarian Lemongrass Soup_____ 80

Salads _____ 82

Asian Noodle and Vegetable Salad _____ 82
Crunchy Coconut-Flavored Salad _____ 83
Cucumber Salad with Lemongrass _____ 83
Fiery Beef Salad _____ 84
Grilled Calamari Salad _____ 85
Papaya Salad _____ 86
Shrimp and Noodle Salad _____ 87
Spicy Rice Salad _____ 88
Spicy Shrimp Salad _____ 89
Sweet-and-Sour Cucumber Salad _____ 90
Thai Dinner Salad _____ 91
Thailand Bamboo Shoots _____ 91
Thailand Seafood Salad _____ 92
Zesty Melon Salad _____ 93

About the Author _____ 94

INTRODUCTION

If you've ever been to an authentic Thai restaurant, you already know that Thai food is all about a delicious balance between the five flavors- sweet, sour, salty, spicy, and bitter. Most recipes contain at least one ingredient for each of these flavors. Once you get used to Thai cooking, you will get a hang of Thai ingredients. You will get a sense of what ingredient does what, and how much of it you like in a particular recipe. You will then see the recipes in this book as a blank canvas, and tweak them to your, or your family's preferences. Let your instincts guide you, once you get a hang of things.

Each dish has a balance of ingredients, but a Thai meal too needs to be balanced as a whole, with a good variety of dishes that complement each other. For instance, if you're cooking a spicy curry, you will do well to serve a plain vegetable stir-fry on the side. It is also common for the Thai dinner table to have a few common taste making condiments so the individuals having the dinner can tweak the flavor of any dish to their liking. For example, vinegar, tamarind water and lime juice are common sour ingredients on the Thai dinner table.

Thai people enjoy food with a wide spectrum of ingredients, including seafood, meat, fruit, and vegetables. Here in Thailand, we like to enjoy what is in season, and what is available at hand in the kitchen. If we're short on an ingredient, we usually improvise.

You might find a few ingredients in this book that are hard to find. When in doubt, google the ingredient, and find a substitution. Some of the greatest recipes in the world are known to us today because someone, somewhere, improvised! So, feel free to improvise yourself. I know you'll need to.

Also, the amount of ingredients used are to my personal taste. Feel free to tweak any taste making ingredient to your own personal taste if you find the flavor too strong or too bland. It is always a good idea to start with less, as more spice can be added later, but it is impossible to remove it once it is in. You'll know the quantities you need to throw in for best results, after you've cooked a recipe once or twice.

Each recipe has "Yield" mentioned at the end. These are approximate, and since we Thai people like to enjoy multiple dishes in one meal, one serving of one dish might not be enough to satiate your hunger. Most recipes in this book are meant to be accompanied by rice.

The most important thing is to enjoy the process of Thai cooking. Follow your instincts, and let your creativity run wild!

WEATHER

Thailand enjoys a monsoon climate. The peninsula has two seasons: wet from November-July, and dry from August-October. The mainland has three seasons: wet from May-November, dry and cool from November-February, and dry and hot from March-April. If you're from a cold country, however, you might say that the weather here is hot and humid all year round.

AGRICULTURE

Thailand's fertile delta region is complemented by its hot and humid climate, yielding perfect agricultural conditions. Some archeologists even believe that central Thailand was the site of the first true agriculture on the planet and that rice has been cultivated there since between 4000 and 3500 B. C. Agricultural products make up 66 percent of the country's exports, and produces more than a third of the world's rice. Other prominent products are coconut, tapioca, rubber, sugar, pineapple, jute, soybeans, and palm oil. Two-thirds of the Thai labor force is engaged in agriculture.

FOOD CULTURE

As we talked before, Thai food is all about balancing sweet, salty, sour, bitter, and hot flavors. Not only the dishes, but the whole meal needs to be balanced with a delicious combinations of all these flavors. A few of the most popular taste makers and flavoring agents in Thai cooking are: coconut, lime, chili, garlic, ginger, cilantro, and dried fish (to make fish sauce). These ingredients are the foundation of Thai flavors.

As with food of any other region, Thai food has a few foreign influences. Chilies were introduced to Asia by the Portuguese in the 16th century, and this hot ingredient became a favorite of the Thai people, and a staple in the Thai kitchen. Hence, the Portuguese have had a huge influence on Thai cuisine. China and their stir-frying cooking techniques too have had a great influence on Thai cuisine. Indian curries and Indonesian spices are quite popular here too.

Thailand enjoys a huge coastline, making seafood a staple. Freshwater fish are super popular here too. Fish sauce is an indispensable part of Thai cuisine, and is used as a sauce, condiment, salt substitute, general taste maker, and flavoring agent. Dried fish are a popular snack in the country.

The country has a tropical climate, which leads to a limitless supply of delicious and exotic fruits and vegetables that are used in pretty much every kind of dish, and sometimes eaten by themselves too. The most important agricultural produce of Thailand is rice. Rice is also the most important and most common ingredient in Thai cuisine. In Thailand, the white and fragrant rice varieties are considered the best. Jasmine rice is a long-grained rice that is one of the favorite varieties here.

Most of the people in Thailand are Theravada Buddhists, and for them killing of animals is forbidden, but eating them is allowed. Regardless, meat is not a very common ingredient in the Thai cuisine, and is considered by most a special and rare treat. The meat that is served is often shredded.

In Thailand, all courses are usually served at once, so that the cook can enjoy the meal with his/her guests. Condiments such as dried chilies, chili paste, chopped peanuts, soy sauce, fish sauce, etc. are present on the table so the diners can tweak the flavor of a dish if they wish to.

Loaded with fish, vegetables, fruits, and rice, and low in meats and dairy, Thai cuisine is one of the healthiest in the world. Thai food is rich in carotinoids, flavonoids, and antioxidative vitamins, all known to have anti-cancer properties. It is no surprise that the Thai have the lowest rates of digestive tract cancer in the world.

THAI COOKING BASICS

Before we dive into the recipes, let us take a look at a few guidelines that might make your cooking experience a little better. These are quite basic, and if you've had some experience of following cookbooks in the past, you can skip them.

1. Read the recipe completely at least once before you start.
2. Make sure you have all the ingredients and tools needed for the recipe ready before you begin.
3. Fresh seasonal ingredients are always best.
4. Do all the cutting, chopping, and weighing the ingredients before you begin cooking.
5. Homemade ingredients are almost always better than store bought ones.
6. When measuring dry ingredients, level them off using the straight edge of a knife.
7. Use standard measuring spoons, cups, etc.

8. Rinse all vegetables and fruits meticulously and pat or spin dry.
9. Take meat out of the fridge approximately 15 minutes before cooking it, letting it come to room temperature. It will cook faster and more uniformly.
10. Use freshly ground pepper, if possible. Pepper starts to lose its flavor and pungency the moment it is ground.

BASIC COOKING METHODS

Here we will discuss a few of the most common cooking methods used in Thai cooking. Thai cooking is usually quite simple, and the methods used here are not much different from those used in the rest of the world.

STIR-FRYING AND SAUTÉING

These are identical cooking techniques that involve cooking in an open pan over high temperatures and with a negligible amount of cooking oil. Sautéing is usually done in either a slope-sided gourmet pan (or frying pan) or a straight-sided sauté pan. Stir-frying done in a wok.

These techniques are great for browning all kinds of meats.

Cooking fats must be relatively tasteless and have a high point. My favorites are canola oil and peanut oil. The oil must but not be smoking before you start to cook. To check, you can drizzle drop or two of water into the pan: It should spatter. Please be cautious as spatters can burn! Shaking the pan for sautéing or swiftly tossing ingredients in stir-frying prevents the food from adhering while it sears.

GRILLING AND BROILING

Grilling and broiling are cooking techniques in which food is cooked by exposing it to direct (often intense) heat over hot coals or some other heat source. This method is usually fast; the direct heat chars surface of the food, imparting delicious flavor to it. The fuel used in a grill impart a nuance of flavor. Adding aromatic wood chips such as or applewood or certain herbs such as lemongrass or fennel will impart additional flavor tones. (This cannot be done when using a broiler.)

The grill can be old fationed, using some type of charcoal, or an electric one. The best grills will allow for fairly controllable heat. To ready your grill for cooking, heat it until hot and then use a long-handled brush to scrape away any residue. Immediately before placing food on the grill, rub a wad of paper towels dipped in oil onto the grate. This will greatly reduce sticking.

Pretty much everything edible can be grilled: soft cuts of meat, poultry, game birds, seafood, fish, or vegetables. The food will grill more uniformly if you let it come to room temperature immediately before cooking. Seasoning, especially with salt, must be done just before you cook, as salt tends to draw out moisture, rendering your final product less juicy. Furthermore, foods that are naturally low in fat must be brushed with oil or butter coated with a sauce to keep them from drying out. Marinades are way to put in additional flavor to grilled foods.

To test when your grilled meat is done, it is best to use an instant-thermometer. If you don't like this method, you can insert the point of a knife to visually see if your food is done. Always bear in mind that your food carries on cooking even after you take it off the grill. Furthermore, meats will reabsorb some of their juices after they are done cooking. Make sure you let your meats rest for 5-10 minutes before you serve.

COOKING IN WATER

Simmering and poaching are both techniques that involve cooking food in liquid. With both techniques, the cooking liquid is first brought a boil and then the heat is decreased in order to reduce bubbling. Poaching should have a little less bubbling action than simmering, but it's hard to tell when something is simmering versus poaching. Some recipes require a covered cooking vessel, others open ones. As something is simmering or poaching, it is vital to skim surface regularly to remove the residue that accumulates. Fish, rice, and poultry all do great with poaching and simmering.

Only a few foods need to be boiled — noodles and potatoes being two of the most common ones. Boiling water is also used to blanch or parboil fruits vegetables before they are moved to another cooking method. Blanching involves placing the ingredients in boiling water for a short period of time and then immersing them into cold water to retain color and flavor or to make it easier to take their skins off. Ingredients that parboiled actually stay in the boiling water a small amount longer, in order to slightly tenderize them.

Another popular cooking technique involving water is steaming. With this method, the ingredients are not immersed in the water, but instead above it on a rack. The pot is covered at all times. Steaming is a very gentle cooking method and it is usually the most healthy. Steamed ingredients do not lose much of their nutrients, texture, or individual flavor. Vegetables and sticky rice do great with steaming.

ROASTING

Roasting is another fundamental cooking method used around the world. A very simple technique that requires an oven, usually with high heat. This technique can also use indirect heat from a grill to obtain similar results. Pretty much everything can be roasted: meats, fishes, vegetables, or fruits.

Roasting meat requires you to season it in some way, sometimes searing it before you place it in your oven and sometimes coating it it cooks — depending on the recipe — and always letting it rest. Resting allows the meat to reabsorb some of its juices, making your roast juicy and easier to carve. To rest your roast, you simply remove it the oven, cover it using foil, and allow it to sit.

A useful gadget to have when roasting is an ovenproof meat thermometer. This will allow you to know when your roast is done to your preference, without cutting into it. For an accurate reading, you must insert tip of the thermometer into the deepest part of the meat without touching bone, fat, or the bottom of the pan. Roasting charts commonly come with the thermometers.

HANDY TOOLS FOR THAI COOKING

KNIFE TYPES AND THEIR USES

- **CHEF'S KNIFE** — a medium-bladed knife used for chopping, cutting, mincing
- **PARING KNIFE** — a short-bladed knife (usually 2 to 4 inches) used trim fruits and vegetables
- **SLICING KNIFE** — a long-bladed knife, either smooth-edged or serrated used for cutting meats or breads

Other useful knives include: boning, utility, cleaver, and fillet.

SPECIALTY UTENSILS

If you're getting started with Thai cooking and don't wish to invest any more cash on fancy tools for the job, you will be able to get by just fine. However, if you want to make your job a little easier, you might want to add a few of these to your kitchen:

- **BLENDER** — great for making sauces and purées
- **CHINOIS** — a sieve perfect for straining stocks, sauces, and purées
- **COLANDER** — perfect for straining noodles
- **FOOD PROCESSOR** — the workhorse of the kitchen when it comes mixing, chopping, puréeing, and shredding
- **HAND BLENDER** — great for making sauces and purées right in the pot
- **MANDOLINE** — an extremely sharp utensil used for precise paper-cutting
- **MORTAR and PESTLE** — a stone container and club used to crush spices and herbs
- **RICE COOKER** — an electric gizmo that takes the guessing out of
- **WOK** — a high-sided, sloping, small-bottomed pan — the quintessential Asian utensil

BASIC FOOD SUBSTITUTIONS

If you're in a country like the USA, you might not be able to find an ingredient that a recipe calls for. When this happens, it is usually a good idea to google the ingredient, and find alternatives you can get your hands on. Below are a few of such ingredients. If you come across more, google is your friend.

THAI INGREDIENT	SUBSTITUTION
Fish sauce	Soy sauce
Cilantro	Parsley
Kaffir lime leaves	Lime peel
Lemongrass	Lemon peel
Rice vinegar	Dry sherry or white vinegar
Long beans	Green beans
Thai eggplant	Green peas
Shallots	Small onions

Homemade curry paste	Store-bought curry paste

DIPPING SAUCES, SALSAS, AND VINAIGRETTES

5-MINUTE DIPPING SAUCE

Ingredients:

- ½ teaspoon dried red pepper flakes
- 1 tablespoon fish sauce
- 1 tablespoon lime juice
- 1 teaspoon minced fresh ginger
- 1 teaspoon sugar

Directions:

1. In a small container, dissolve the sugar in 1 tablespoon of water.
2. Mix in the rest of the ingredients; tweak seasonings if required. Serve at room temperature.

Yield: Approximately 4 tablespoons

BANANA, TAMARIND, AND MINT SALSA

Ingredients:

- ¼ cup Tamarind Concentrate (Page 29)
- 1 roasted red jalapeño, seeded and chopped
- 1 tablespoon chopped fresh mint
- 1 tablespoon lime juice
- 1 teaspoon brown sugar
- 4 ripe bananas, peeled and finely diced

Directions:

1. Lightly fold all the ingredients together.

Yield: Approximately 2 cups

This unique salsa goes perfectly with roasted or grilled poultry or game.

GINGER-LEMONGRASS VINAIGRETTE

Ingredients:

- ¼ cup grated fresh gingerroot
- 1 quart rice wine vinegar
- 2 stalks lemongrass, outer leaves removed and discarded, inner core slightly mashed

Directions:

1. Mix all the ingredients in a nonreactive pot and simmer using low heat for half an hour.
2. Turn off the heat and allow it to stand overnight. Strain before you serve.

Yield: Approximately 1 quart

JALAPEÑO-LIME VINAIGRETTE

Ingredients:

- 1 cup vegetable or canola oil
- 1 jalapeño, seeded and chopped
- 1 tablespoon sugar
- 1 cup lime juice
- Salt and pepper to taste

Directions:

1. Put the jalapeño, lime juice, sugar, and salt and pepper in a food processor; blend for a minute.
2. While continuing to blend, slowly put in the oil; blend for half a minute or until well blended.

Yield: Approximately 1 cups

MANGO-CUCUMBER SALSA

Ingredients:

- ¼ cup cut green onion
- ¼ cup orange juice
- 1 firm, ripe mango, peeled, seeded, and slice into ¼-inch dice
- 1 medium cucumber, seeded and slice into ¼-inch dice
- 1 teaspoon vegetable oil
- 2 teaspoons lime juice
- Salt and pepper to taste

Directions:

1. Mix all the ingredients in a small container.

Yield: Approximately 2 cups

MANGO-PINEAPPLE SALSA

Ingredients:

- ¼ cup snipped chives
- ½ cup diced red onion
- 1 cup diced pineapple
- 1 cup mango pieces
- 1 cup seeded and chopped tomato
- 1 serrano chili, seeded and chopped
- 2 tablespoons lime juice
- 2 tablespoons vegetable oil Salt and pepper to taste
- 3 tablespoons chopped cilantro

Directions:

1. Mix all the ingredients in a small container.
2. Cover and place in your fridge for minimum 2 hours before you serve.

Yield: Approximately 4 cups

MINT-CILANTRO "CHUTNEY"

Ingredients:

- ½ teaspoon minced honey
- ¾ cup packed cilantro
- ¾ cup packed mint leaves
- 2 teaspoons honey
- 3 tablespoons sour cream
- 1 cup unsalted peanuts, toasted
- Salt and pepper to taste

Directions:

1. Put the peanuts in a food processor and finely grind.
2. Put in the rest of the ingredients to the processor and blend until well blended.

Yield: Approximately 2 cups

MINTY DIPPING SAUCE

Ingredients:

- ¼ cup chopped mint leaves
- ¼ cup lime juice
- 1 serrano chili, seeded and diced
- 1 tablespoon grated lime zest
- 2 cloves garlic, minced
- 2 tablespoons fish sauce

Directions:

1. Put all the ingredients in a blender and process until the desired smoothness is achieved.
2. Serve with a variety of grilled, skewered meats and raw or blanched vegetables.

Yield: Approximately 1 cup

PEANUT DIPPING SAUCE — 1

Ingredients:

- ¼ cup chicken or vegetable stock
- ¼ cup heavy cream
- ¼ cup lemon juice
- 1 teaspoon grated gingerroot
- 1½ cups coconut milk
- 2 tablespoons brown sugar
- 2 tablespoons soy sauce
- 3–4 dashes (or to taste) Tabasco
- 4 cloves garlic, pressed
- 1 cup crispy peanut butter

Directions:

1. Mix the peanut butter, coconut milk, lemon juice, soy sauce, brown sugar, ginger, garlic, and Tabasco in a small deep cooking pan on moderate heat. Cook while stirring continuously, until the sauce has the consistency of heavy cream, approximately fifteen minutes.
2. Move the mixture to a blender and purée for a short period of time.
3. Put in the stock and cream, and blend until the desired smoothness is achieved.

Yield: Approximately 2 cups

PEANUT DIPPING SAUCE — 2

Ingredients:

- ¼ cup fresh lime juice
- ¼ cup half-and-half or heavy cream
- ¼ cup low-sodium beef broth

- 1 teaspoon grated gingerroot
- 1½ cups unsweetened canned coconut milk
- 2 tablespoons brown sugar
- 2 tablespoons soy sauce
- 2 teaspoons minced garlic Ground cayenne or crushed red pepper flakes to taste
- 1 cup crispy peanut butter

Directions:

1. In a moderate-sized-sized deep cooking pan, mix the peanut butter, coconut milk, lime juice, soy sauce, brown sugar, ginger, garlic, and cayenne.
2. Stirring continuously, cook on moderate heat until the sauce thickens, approximately fifteen minutes.
3. Take away the sauce from the heat and put in the beef broth and cream. Using a hand mixer, blend until the desired smoothness is achieved. Heat for a short period of time just prior to serving.

Yield: Approximately 2 cups

PEANUT DIPPING SAUCE — 3

Ingredients:

- ½ cup smooth peanut butter
- 1 cup canned coconut milk
- 1 tablespoon fish sauce
- 1 teaspoon fresh lemon juice
- 1 teaspoon Tabasco
- 2 tablespoons fresh lime juice
- 2 teaspoons light brown sugar
- 2 teaspoons soy sauce
- 3 shallots

Directions:

1. Roast the shallots in an oven preheated to 325 degrees for approximately five minutes or until tender. Allow them to cool to roughly room temperature.
2. Put all ingredients in a blender or food processor and pulse until the desired smoothness is achieved.

Yield: Approximately 2 cups

PEANUT PESTO

Ingredients:

- ¼ cup honey
- ¼ teaspoon (or to taste) red pepper flakes
- ½ cup sesame oil
- ½ cup soy sauce
- 1 cup unsalted roasted peanuts
- 2–3 cloves garlic, minced
- 1 cup water

Directions:

1. Put the peanuts in a food processor fitted using a metal blade; pulse until fine.
2. While continuing to blend, put in the rest of the ingredients one by one through the feed tube until well mixed.

Yield: Approximately 2 cups

QUICK HOT DIPPING SAUCE

Ingredients:

- ½ cup white vinegar
- 1 loaded tablespoon prepared chili-garlic sauce

Directions:

1. Mix the 2 ingredients before you serve.

Yield: Approximately ½ cup

SPICY THAI DRESSING

Ingredients:

- 1 fresh red cayenne pepper or
- 1 tablespoon plus 1 teaspoon rice wine vinegar
- 1 tablespoon sesame oil
- 1 teaspoon grated gingerroot
- 1 teaspoon sugar
- 2 cloves garlic
- 2 tablespoons soy sauce
- 2 Thai peppers, stemmed, seeded, and slice into pieces
- 3 tablespoons water

Directions:

1. Put all the ingredients in a blender and process until the desired smoothness is achieved.

Yield: Approximately 1 cup

SWEET-AND-SOUR DIPPING SAUCE

Ingredients:

- ½ cup white vinegar
- ½ teaspoon salt
- 1 cup sugar
- 1 loaded tablespoon prepared chili-garlic sauce

Directions:

1. Mix the vinegar, sugar, and salt in a small deep cooking pan on moderate to high heat; bring to its boiling point, reduce to a simmer, and cook for eight to ten minutes, stirring once in a while.

2. Mix in the chili sauce and turn off the heat. Allow to cool to room temperature before you serve.

Yield: Approximately 1½ cups

THAI-STYLE PLUM DIPPING SAUCE

Ingredients:

- 2 tablespoons honey Tabasco to taste
- 1 cup plum preserves
- 1 cup water
- 1 cup white vinegar

Directions:

1. Put all the ingredients apart from the Tabasco in a food processor or blender, and process until the desired smoothness is achieved.
2. Move the mixture to a small deep cooking pan and bring to its boiling point on moderate heat; decrease the heat and simmer until thick, approximately twelve to fifteen minutes.
3. Allow to cool completely, then mix in the Tabasco.

Yield: Approximately 2 cups

THAI CURRY PASTES, MARINADES, AND OTHER CONCOCTIONS

ASIAN MARINADE — 1

Ingredients:

- ¼ cup fish sauce
- ¼ cup soy sauce (if possible low-sodium)
- ½ cup freshly squeezed lime juice
- 1 tablespoon curry powder
- 1 tablespoon light brown sugar
- 1 teaspoon minced garlic Crushed dried red pepper
- 2 tablespoons crispy peanut butter

Directions:

1. Mix all the ingredients in a blender or food processor and pulse until the desired smoothness is achieved.

Yield: Approximately 1¼ cups

ASIAN MARINADE — 2

Ingredients:

- ¼ cup chopped green onion
- ¼ cup soy sauce
- ¼ teaspoon ground anise
- ½ cup lime juice
- 1 tablespoon freshly grated gingerroot
- 1 tablespoon honey
- 1 teaspoon Chinese 5-spice powder

- 2 tablespoons hoisin sauce
- 2 tablespoons sesame oil
- 3 cloves garlic, minced
- 3 tablespoons chopped cilantro
- 1 cup vegetable oil

Directions:

1. Mix the lime juice, soy sauce, hoisin sauce, and honey, and blend thoroughly.
2. Slowly whisk in the vegetable and sesame oils. Put in the rest of the ingredients and mix meticulously.

Yield: Approximately 1¼ cups

This recipe has a definite Chinese influence, featuring soy sauce, hoisin sauce, 5-spice powder, and sesame oil.

BLACK BEAN PASTE

Ingredients:

- 1 medium to big onion, minced
- 1 tablespoon fish sauce
- 1 teaspoon brown sugar
- 2 cloves garlic, chopped
- 2 jalapeños, seeded and chopped
- 2 tablespoons vegetable oil
- 2 teaspoons lime juice
- 3 green onions, trimmed and cut
- 4 tablespoons canned black beans or black soy beans

Directions:

1. In a moderate-sized-sized sauté pan, heat the oil over moderate-the onions, jalapeños, garlic, and green onions, and sauté onion becomes translucent.

2. Using a slotted spoon, move the sautéed vegetables to processor or blender (set aside the oil in the sauté pan). rest of the ingredients and process for a short period of time to create a not-paste.
3. Reheat the reserved oil in the sauté pan. Move the paste and heat for five minutes, stirring continuously. If the paste seems thick, add a small amount of water.

Yield: Approximately ½ cup

CHILI TAMARIND PASTE

Ingredients:

- ½ cup dried shrimp
- 1 cup cut shallots
- 1 tablespoon fish sauce
- 1¾ cups vegetable oil, divided
- 12 small Thai chilies or
- 3 tablespoons brown sugar
- 3 tablespoons Tamarind Concentrate (Page 29)
- 6 serrano chilies
- 1 cup garlic

Directions:

1. Put the dried shrimp in a small container. Cover the shrimp stir for a short period of time, and drain; set aside.
2. Pour 1½ cups of the vegetable oil in a moderate-sized deep cooking pan. the oil to roughly 360 degrees on moderate to high heat.
3. Put in the garlic and fry until a golden-brown colour is achieved. Using a slotted move the garlic to a container lined using paper towels.
4. Put in the shallots to the deep cooking pan and fry for two to three minutes; the shallots to the container with the garlic.
5. Fry the reserved shrimp in the deep cooking pan for a couple of minutes; the container.
6. Fry the chilies until they become brittle, approximately half a minute; them to the container. (Allow oil to cool completely discarding.)

7. Mix the fried ingredients, the rest of the oil, and the a food processor; process to make a smooth paste.
8. Put the paste in a small deep cooking pan on moderate heat. Put in the sugar and fish sauce, and cook, stirring once in a while, for approximately five minutes.
9. Allow the paste to return to room temperature before placing in an airtight container.

Yield: Approximately 3 cups

CHILI VINEGAR

Ingredients:

- ½ cup white vinegar
- 2 teaspoons fish sauce
- 3 serrano chilies, seeded and finely cut

Directions:

1. Put all of the ingredients in a container.
2. Allow to sit minimum twenty minutes to allow the flavors to develop.

Yield: Approximately ½ cup

COCONUT MARINADE

Ingredients:

- ¼–½ teaspoon red chili pepper flakes
- 1 tablespoon grated lime zest
- 1 tablespoon minced fresh ginger
- 2 tablespoons shredded, unsweetened coconut
- 2 teaspoons sugar
- 3 tablespoons lime juice
- 3 tablespoons rice wine vinegar
- teaspoon curry powder

Directions:

1. Warm the vinegar using low heat. Put in the coconut and ginger to become tender.
2. Turn off the heat and mix in the rest of the ingredients.

Yield: Approximately ½ cup

GREEN CURRY PASTE — 1

Ingredients:

- ¼ cup vegetable oil
- ½ cup chopped cilantro
- ½ teaspoon ground cloves
- ½ teaspoon shrimp paste
- 1 (1½-inch) piece gingerroot, peeled and chopped
- 1 stalk lemongrass, tough outer leaves removed, inner soft portion chopped
- 1 teaspoon black pepper
- 1 teaspoon ground cumin
- 1 teaspoon salt
- 10 green serrano chilies
- 2 teaspoons grated lime zest
- 2 teaspoons ground coriander
- 2 teaspoons ground nutmeg
- 3 shallots, crudely chopped
- 5 cloves garlic

Directions:

1. Put the first 6 ingredients in a food processor and process mixed. Put in the rest of the ingredients, apart from the vegetable process until the desired smoothness is achieved.
2. Slowly put in the oil until a thick paste May be placed in the fridge up to 4 weeks.

Yield: 1 cup

GREEN CURRY PASTE — 2

Ingredients:

- 1 (1-inch) piece ginger, peeled and chopped
- 1 medium onion, chopped
- 1 teaspoon salt
- 1 teaspoon shrimp paste
- 2 green bell peppers, seeded and chopped
- 2 tablespoons vegetable oil
- 2 teaspoons chopped lemongrass
- 2 teaspoons cumin seeds, toasted
- 2–4 green jalapeño chilies, seeded and chopped
- 3 cloves garlic, chopped
- 3 tablespoons coriander seeds, toasted
- 3 teaspoons water
- 4 tablespoons chopped cilantro
- 4 tablespoons Tamarind Concentrate (Page 29)

Directions:

1. Put all the ingredients in a food processor and pulse until the desired smoothness is achieved. Move to a small deep cooking pan and bring to a simmer on moderate to low heat. Decrease the heat to low and cook, stirring regularly, for five minutes.
2. Mix in 1 cup of water and bring the mixture to its boiling point. Decrease the heat, cover, and simmer for half an hour

Yield: Approximately 1 cup

LEMON CHILI VINEGAR

Ingredients:

- 1 quart white wine vinegar Peel of 4 limes
- 8–10 serrano chilies

Directions:

1. Mix all the ingredients in a moderate-sized deep cooking pan and bring to a simmer on moderate heat.
2. Decrease the heat and simmer for about ten minutes.
3. Cool to room temperature, then strain.

Yield: Approximately 1 quart

LEMONGRASS MARINADE

Ingredients:

- ¼ tablespoon soy sauce
- 1 cup extra-virgin olive oil
- 1 jalapeño chili pepper, seeded and chopped
- 1 tablespoon fish sauce
- 2 cloves garlic, minced
- 2 stalks lemongrass, trimmed and smashed
- 2 tablespoons chopped cilantro
- 2 tablespoons lime juice

Directions:

1. Pour the olive oil into a pan and heat until warm.
2. Put in the lemongrass and garlic, and cook for a minute. Turn off the heat and let cool completely.
3. Mix in the rest of the ingredients.

Yield: Approximately 1 cups

MALAYSIAN MARINADE

Ingredients:

- ¼ cup chopped cilantro

- ¼ cup soy sauce
- ¼ cup vegetable oil
- ½ teaspoon coriander
- ½ teaspoon ground cumin
- 1 green onion, trimmed and thinly cut
- 1 teaspoon grated lime zest
- 2 tablespoons grated gingerroot
- 2 tablespoons honey
- 3 tablespoons lime juice

Directions:

1. Mix the honey, lime juice, lime zest, and soy sauce in a small container.
2. Slowly whisk in the oil.
3. Mix in the rest of the ingredients.

Yield: Approximately 1 cup

MINTY TAMARIND PASTE

Ingredients:

- ¼ cup peanuts
- ½ cup Tamarind Concentrate (Page 29)
- 1 bunch cilantro leaves
- 1 bunch mint leaves
- 4–5 Thai bird peppers or 2 serrano chilies, seeded and chopped

Directions:

1. Put all the ingredients in a food processor and pulse to make a paste.

Yield: Approximately 2 cups

NORTHERN (OR JUNGLE) CURRY PASTE

Ingredients:

- ¼ cup chopped arugula
- ¼ cup chopped chives
- ½ cup chopped mint
- 1 (3-inch) piece ginger, peeled and chopped
- 1 cup chopped basil
- 1 stalk lemongrass, tough outer leaves removed and discarded, inner core minced
- 1 tablespoon shrimp paste
- 12 serrano chilies, seeded and chopped
- 2 tablespoons vegetable oil
- 4 shallots, chopped
- 6–8 Thai bird chilies, seeded and chopped

Directions:

1. In a moderate-sized-sized sauté pan, heat the oil on medium. Put in shrimp paste, lemongrass, ginger, and shallots, and sauté until shallots start to turn translucent and the mixture is very aromatic.
2. Move the mixture to a food processor and pulse until adding 1 or 2 tablespoons of water to help with the grinding.
3. Put in the rest of the ingredients and more water if required to pulse until crudely mixed.

Yield: Approximately 2 cups

RED CURRY PASTE — 1

Ingredients:

- 1 (½-inch) piece ginger, finely chopped
- 1 medium onion, chopped
- 1 stalk lemongrass, outer leaves removed and discarded, inner core finely chopped
- 1 teaspoon salt
- 2 garlic cloves, chopped
- 2 tablespoons Tamarind Concentrate (Page 29)

- 2 teaspoons cumin seeds, toasted
- 2 teaspoons paprika
- 3 kaffir lime leaves or the peel of 1 lime, chopped
- 3 tablespoons coriander seeds, toasted
- 3 tablespoons vegetable oil
- 4 tablespoons water
- 6–8 red serrano chilies, seeded and chopped

Directions:

1. Put all the ingredients in a food processor and pulse until super smooth.
2. Move to a small deep cooking pan and bring to a simmer on moderate to low heat. Decrease the heat to low and cook, stirring regularly, for five minutes.
3. Mix in 1 cup of water and bring the mixture to its boiling point. Decrease the heat, cover, and simmer thirty minutes.

Yield: Approximately ½ cup

RED CURRY PASTE — 2

Ingredients:

- 1 (2-inch) piece ginger, peeled and thoroughly minced
- 1 small onion, chopped
- 2 cloves garlic, minced
- 2 stalks lemongrass, tough outer leaves removed and discarded, inner core thoroughly minced
- 2 tablespoons ground turmeric
- 3 big dried red California chilies, seeded and chopped
- 5 dried Thai bird or similar chilies, seeded and chopped

Directions:

1. Put the chilies in a container and cover them with hot water. Allow to stand for minimum 30 minutes. Drain the chilies, saving for later 1 cup of the soaking liquid.

2. Put all the ingredients and 2–3 tablespoons of the soaking liquid in a food processor. Process to make a thick, smooth paste. Put in additional liquid if required.

Yield: Approximately 1 cup

SHREDDED FRESH COCONUT

Ingredients:

- 1 heavy coconut, with liquid

Directions:

1. Preheat your oven to 400 degrees.
2. Pierce the eye of the coconut using a metal skewer or screwdriver and drain the coconut water (reserve it for later use if you prefer).
3. Bake the coconut for fifteen minutes, then remove and allow to cool.
4. When the coconut is sufficiently cool to handle, use a hammer to break the shell. Using the tip of a knife, cautiously pull the flesh from the shell. Remove any remaining brown membrane with a vegetable peeler.
5. Shred the coconut using a 4-sided grater. Fresh coconut will keep in your fridge for maximum one week.

Yield: Approximately 1 cup

SOUTHERN (OR MASSAMAN) CURRY PASTE

Ingredients:

- ¼ teaspoon ground cinnamon
- ¼ teaspoon whole black peppercorns
- ½ teaspoon cardamom seeds, toasted
- 1 (1-inch) piece ginger, peeled and minced
- 1 stalk lemongrass, tough outer leaves removed and discarded, inner core finely chopped
- 1 teaspoon lime peel
- 1 teaspoon salt

- 1 teaspoon shrimp paste (not necessary)
- 2 tablespoons coriander seeds, toasted
- 2 tablespoons vegetable oil
- 2 teaspoons brown sugar
- 2 teaspoons cumin seeds, toasted
- 2 whole cloves
- 3 tablespoons Tamarind Concentrate (Page 29)
- 3 tablespoons water
- 6–8 big dried red chilies (often called California chilies), soaked in hot water for five minutes and drained

Directions:

1. Put all ingredients in a food processor and pulse until the desired smoothness is achieved.
2. Move to a small deep cooking pan and bring to a simmer on moderate to low heat. Decrease the heat to low and cook, stirring regularly, for five minutes.
3. Mix in 1 cup of water and bring the mixture to its boiling point. Decrease the heat, cover, and simmer thirty minutes.

Yield: Approximately 1 cup

TAMARIND CONCENTRATE

Ingredients:

- 1 cup warm water
- 2 ounces seedless tamarind pulp (sold in Asian markets)

Directions:

1. Put the tamarind pulp and water in a small container for about twenty minutes or until the pulp is tender.
2. Break the pulp apart using the backside of a spoon and stir until blended.
3. Pour the mixture through a fine-mesh sieve, pushing the tender pulp through the strainer. Discard any fibrous pulp remaining in the strainer.

Yield: Approximately 1 cup

TAMARIND MARINADE

Ingredients:

- ¼ cup fresh lime juice
- ¼ cup toasted, unsweetened coconut
- ¼ cup vegetable oil
- ½ cup chopped cilantro leaves
- 1 shallot, chopped
- 1 tablespoon brown sugar
- 1 tablespoon diced fresh gingerroot
- 1 tablespoon soy sauce
- 1½ cups Tamarind Concentrate (Page 29)
- 2 garlic cloves, minced
- 4 pieces lime peel (roughly ½-inch by two-inches)

Directions:

1. Mix the tamarind and lime peel in a small deep cooking pan and bring to a simmer; cook for five minutes.
2. Turn off the heat and cool completely. Mix in the rest of the ingredients.

Yield: Approximately 2 cups

THAI GRILLING RUB

Ingredients:

- 1 teaspoon dried lime peel
- 1 teaspoon freshly ground black pepper
- 1 teaspoon ground ginger
- 4 teaspoons salt

Directions:

1. Mix all the ingredients and mix meticulously. Store in an airtight container.
2. To use, wash the meat of your choice under cool water and pat dry; drizzle the meat with the spice mixture (to taste) and rub it in together with some olive oil, then grill or broil to your preference.

Yield: Approximately

THAI MARINADE — 1

Ingredients:

- ¼ cup chopped cilantro
- ¼ cup fresh lime juice
- ¼ teaspoon hot pepper flakes
- ½ cup sesame oil
- 1 big stalk lemongrass, crushed
- 1 tablespoon brown sugar
- 2 tablespoons chopped peanuts
- 2 tablespoons fish sauce
- 3 cloves garlic, minced

Directions:

1. Mix the fish sauce and lime juice in a small container.
2. Slowly whisk in the sesame oil, then mix in rest of the ingredients.

Yield: Approximately 1 cup

THAI MARINADE — 2

Ingredients:

- ¼ cup chopped basil leaves
- ¼ cup chopped mint leaves

- ¼ cup peanut oil
- ½ cup rice wine
- 1 small onion, chopped
- 1 tablespoon chopped gingerroot
- 1 tablespoon sweet soy sauce
- 2 tablespoons chopped lemongrass
- 3 cloves garlic, minced
- 3 tablespoons fish sauce

Directions:

1. Mix the fish sauce, sweet soy sauce, and the rice wine in a small container.
2. Slowly whisk in the peanut oil, then mix in rest of the ingredients.

Yield: Approximately 1½ cups

THAI MARINADE — 3

Ingredients:

- ¼ cup chopped cilantro leaves
- ¼ cup lime juice
- ½ cup Red Curry Paste (see recipes on pages 4 and 5)
- 1 (12-ounce) can coconut milk
- 1 stalk lemongrass, roughly chopped
- 1 tablespoon sweet soy sauce
- 1 teaspoon fresh gingerroot, chopped
- 2 tablespoons fish sauce
- 6 kaffir lime leaves, finely cut

Directions:

1. Mix the coconut milk, curry paste, lemongrass, and kaffir leaves in a small deep cooking pan; bring to a simmer on moderate heat.
2. Decrease the heat and carry on simmering for fifteen minutes.

3. Turn off the heat and let cool to room temperature.
4. Mix in all the rest of the ingredients.

Yield: Approximately 2 cups

THAI VINEGAR MARINADE

Ingredients:

- ¼ cup chopped lemongrass
- 1 tablespoon fresh grated gingerroot
- 1 tablespoon sugar
- 2–3 tablespoons vegetable oil
- 3 tablespoons chopped green onion
- 3½ cups rice wine vinegar
- 4 cloves garlic, minced
- 6 dried red chilies, seeded and crumbled

Directions:

1. Put the garlic, chilies, green onions, and ginger in a food processor or blender and process to make a paste.
2. Heat the oil in a wok or frying pan, put in the paste, and stir-fry for four to five minutes. Turn off the heat and allow the mixture to cool completely.
3. In a small deep cooking pan, bring the vinegar to its boiling point. Put in the sugar and the lemongrass; decrease the heat and simmer for about twenty minutes.
4. Mix in the reserved paste.

Yield: Approximately 3 cups

YELLOW BEAN SAUCE

Ingredients:

- 1 (½-inch) piece ginger, peeled and chopped

- 1 medium to big onion, minced
- 1 teaspoon ground coriander
- 2 serrano chilies, seeded and chopped
- 2 tablespoons lime juice
- 2 tablespoons vegetable oil
- 2 tablespoons water
- 4 tablespoons fermented yellow beans (fermented soy beans)

Directions:

1. In a moderate-sized-sized sauté pan, heat the oil on moderate heat. Put in the onion and chilies, and sauté until the onion becomes translucent. Mix in the ginger and coriander, and carry on cooking for half a minute.
2. Put in the beans, lime juice, and water, and simmer using low heat for about ten minutes.
3. Move the mixture to a blender and process until the desired smoothness is achieved.

Yield: Approximately 1 cup

DESSERTS

BANANA COCONUT SOUP

Ingredients:

- 1 cinnamon stick
- 1 tablespoon lemon juice
- 2 tablespoons minced gingerroot
- 4 cups banana slices, plus extra for decoration
- 4 cups canned coconut milk
- Salt to taste

Directions:

1. In a big deep cooking pan, bring the coconut milk to its boiling point. Put in the banana, ginger, cinnamon stick, lemon juice, and a pinch of salt. Decrease the heat and simmer for ten to fifteen minutes or until the banana is very tender.
2. Take away the cinnamon stick and let cool slightly.
3. Using a handheld blender (or a blender or food processor), purée the soup until the desired smoothness is achieved.
4. Serve the soup in preheated bowls, decorated with banana slices and coconut.

Yield: Servings 6–8

BANANAS POACHED IN COCONUT MILK

Ingredients:

- ¼ teaspoon salt
- 1 cup sugar
- 2–3 small, slightly green bananas
- 4 cups coconut milk

Directions:

1. Peel the bananas and slice them in half along the length.
2. Pour the coconut milk into a pan big enough to hold the bananas laid flat in a single layer. Put in the sugar and salt and bring to its boiling point.
3. Reduce the heat, put in the bananas, and simmer until the bananas are just warmed through, approximately 3 to five minutes.
4. Serve the bananas warm on small plates decorated with fresh coconut and pineapple wedges.

Yield: Servings 2–3

CITRUS FOOL

Ingredients:

- ½ cup heavy cream
- ½ cup orange, lime, or lemon juice
- 1 big egg, beaten
- 2 (3-inch-long, ½-inch wide) strips of citrus zest, minced
- 3 tablespoons sugar
- 3 tablespoons unsalted butter

Directions:

1. Put the juice in a small deep cooking pan. Over moderate to high heat, reduce the liquid by half.
2. Take away the pan from the heat and mix in the sugar and butter. Mix in the egg until well blended.
3. Return the pan to the burner and cook on medium-low heat for three to five minutes or until bubbles barely start to form.
4. Take away the pan from the heat and mix in the citrus zest. Put the pan in a container of ice and stir the mixture until it is cold.
5. In another container, whip the cream until firm. Fold the citrus mixture meticulously into the cream.

Yield: Servings 4

COCONUT CUSTARD

Ingredients:

- 1 (16-ounce) can coconut cream
- 3 tablespoons butter
- 6 big eggs, lightly beaten
- 1 cup fine granulated sugar
- Fresh tropical fruit (not necessary)

Directions:

1. In a large, heavy-bottomed deep cooking pan, mix together the coconut cream and the sugar.
2. Over moderate heat, cook and stir the mixture until the sugar is thoroughly blended.
3. Lower the heat to low and mix in the eggs. Cook while stirring once in a while, until the mixture is thick and coats the back of a spoon, approximately ten to twelve minutes.
4. Take away the pan from the heat and put in the butter. Stir until the butter is completely melted and blended.
5. Pour the custard into six 4-ounce custard cups. Put the cups in a baking pan. Pour boiling water into the baking pan until it comes midway up the sides of the custard cups.
6. Cautiously move the baking pan to a preheated 325-degree oven. Bake the custards for thirty to forty minutes until set. (The tip of a knife should come out clean when inserted into the middle of the custard.)
7. Serve warm or at room temperature. Decorate using chopped tropical fruit, if you wish.

Yield: Servings 6

COCONUT-PINEAPPLE SOUFFLÉ FOR 2

Ingredients:

- ½ cup (½-inch) cubes ladyfingers or sponge cake

- 1 egg yolk
- 2 egg whites
- 2 tablespoons dark rum
- 2 tablespoons finely chopped fresh pineapple
- 2 tablespoons sugar
- 2½ tablespoons grated sweetened coconut
- Lemon juice
- Softened butter for the molds
- Sugar for the molds

Directions:

1. Preheat your oven to 400 degrees.
2. Butter 2-¾ or 1-cup soufflée molds and then drizzle them with sugar. Place in your fridge the molds until ready to use.
3. Put the ladyfinger cubes in a small container. Pour the rum over the cubes and allow to soak for five minutes.
4. Squeeze the juice from the pineapple, saving both the pulp and 1 tablespoon of the juice.
5. In a small container, beat the egg yolk with the pineapple juice until very thick. Fold in the cake cubes, pineapple pulp, and coconut.
6. In another small container, beat the egg whites with a few drops of lemon juice until foamy. Slowly put in the 2 tablespoons of sugar, while continuing to beat until the whites are stiff and shiny.
7. Lightly fold the pineapple mixture into the egg whites.
8. Ladle the batter into the prepared molds and bake for eight to ten minutes or until puffy and mildly browned.

Yield: 2

CRISPY CREPES WITH FRESH FRUIT

Ingredients:

- ¼ cup shredded, unsweetened coconut
- 1 cup heavy cream

- 1 package frozen puff pastry sheets, thawed in accordance with package instructions
- 1 tablespoon unflavored rum or coconut-flavored rum
- 2 cups raspberries, blueberries, or other fresh fruit, the best 12 berries reserved for decoration
- 2 tablespoons confectioner's sugar, divided

Directions:

1. Preheat your oven to 400 degrees.
2. Put the puff pastry sheet on a work surface and slice into 12 equalsized pieces. Put the pastry pieces on a baking sheet.
3. Bake the pastry roughly ten minutes. Take out of the oven and use a sifter to shake a small amount of the confectioner?s sugar over the puff pastry. Return to the oven and carry on baking for roughly five minutes or until golden. Put the puff pastry on a wire rack and let cool completely.
4. Put the berries in a food processor and for a short period of time process to make a rough purée.
5. Whip the cream with the rest of the confectioner's sugar until thick, but not firm. Mix in the coconut and the rum.
6. To serve, place 1 piece of puff pastry in the center of each serving plate, spoon some cream over the pastry, and then top with some purée. Put another pastry on top, decorate with some of the rest of the berries, any remaining juice from the purée, and a drizzle of confectioner's sugar.

FRESH ORANGES IN ROSE WATER

Ingredients:

- 1½ cups sugar
- 3 cups water
- 4–6 teaspoons rose water
- 8 oranges

Directions:

1. Peel and segment the oranges. Put them in a container, cover, and set aside in your fridge.
2. In a deep cooking pan, bring the water and the sugar to its boiling point over moderatehigh heat. Boil gently for fifteen to 20 or until the mixture becomes syrupy. Turn off the heat and mix in the rose water. Allow to cool to room temperature and then place in your fridge
3. To serve, place orange segments in individual dessert cups. Pour rose water syrup over the top.

Yield: Servings 6–8

LEMONGRASS CUSTARD

Ingredients:

- ½ cup suga
- 2 cups whole milk
- 2 stalks fresh lemongrass, finely chopped (soft inner portion only)
- 6 egg yolks

Directions:

1. Preheat your oven to 275 degrees.
2. In a moderate-sized-sized deep cooking pan, on moderate to high heat, bring the milk and the lemongrass to its boiling point. Lower the heat and simmer for five minutes. Cover the milk mixture, remove the heat, and allow it to sit for about ten minutes on the burner.
3. In a mixing container, beat the egg yolks with the sugar until thick.
4. Strain the milk mixture through a fine-mesh sieve, then slowly pour it into the egg yolks, whisking continuously.
5. Split the mixture between 6 small custard cups and put the cups in a high-sided baking or roasting pan. Put in warm water to the pan so that it reaches to roughly an inch below the top of the custard cups. Cover the pan firmly using foil.
6. Put the pan in your oven and bake for roughly twenty minutes or until the custards are set on the sides but still slightly wobbly in the middle.

Yield: Servings 6

MANGO FOOL

Ingredients:

- ¼ cup sugar
- 1 cup heavy cream
- 1 tablespoon confectioners' sugar
- 2 ripe mangoes, peeled and flesh cut from the pits 2 tablespoons lime juice
- Crystallized ginger (not necessary)
- Mint leaves (not necessary)

Directions:

1. Put the mangoes in a food processor with the lime juice and sugar. Puréee until the desired smoothness is achieved.
2. In a big container beat the heavy cream with the confectioners' sugar until firm.
3. Thoroughly fold the mango purée into the heavy cream.
4. Serve in goblets decorated with crystallized ginger or sprigs of mint, if you wish.

Yield: Servings 4–6

MANGO SAUCE OVER ICE CREAM

Ingredients:

- 1 banana, peeled and chopped
- 1 tablespoon brandy (not necessary)
- 2 mangoes, peeled, pitted, and diced
- 1 cup (or to taste) sugar
- Juice of 2 big limes (or to taste)
- Vanilla ice cream

Directions:

1. In a moderate-sized-sized deep cooking pan using low heat, simmer the mangoes, banana, sugar, and lime juice for thirty minutes, stirring regularly.

2. Put in the brandy and simmer 5 more minutes.
3. Turn off the heat and let cool slightly or to room temperature.
4. To serve, scoop ice cream into individual serving bowls. Ladle sauce over top.

Yield: 2 cups

PINEAPPLE RICE

Ingredients:

- ¼ cup sugar
- ½ cup short-grained rice
- 1 ripe pineapple
- 2 teaspoons chopped crystallized ginger, divided
- 3 tablespoons roasted cashew nuts, chopped
- Pinch of salt
- Zest and juice of 1 lemon

Directions:

1. Chop the pineapple in half along the length, leaving the leaves undamaged on 1 side. Scoop out the pineapple flesh of both halves, leaving a ½-inch edge on the half with the leaves. Dice the pineapple fruit from 1 half and purée the fruit from the other half in a food processor together with the sugar and salt; set aside.
2. Strain the fruit purée through a fine-mesh sieve into a measuring cup. Put in enough water to make 1¾ cups. Move to a small deep cooking pan and bring to its boiling point on moderate to high heat.
3. Wash and drain the rice. Mix the rice into the pineapple purée. Mix in the lemon zest, lemon juice, and 1 teaspoon of the ginger. Bring to its boiling point; reduce heat, cover, and simmer until the liquid has been absorbed, approximately twenty minutes.
4. Combine the reserved pineapple cubes into the rice.
5. To serve, spoon the rice into the hollowed out pineapple that has the leaves. Decorate using the rest of the ginger and the roasted cashews.

Yield: Servings 4–6

PINEAPPLE-MANGO SHERBET

Ingredients:

- ½ cup plain yogurt
- 1 big orange, peeled and segmented
- 1 cup pineapple pieces
- 1 tablespoon lime zest
- 1 teaspoon orange-flavored liqueur (not necessary)
- 2 mangoes, peeled, pitted, and slice into 1-inch cubes
- 1 cup sugar

Directions:

1. Put the orange segments, mango cubes, and pineapple pieces on a baking sheet lined with waxed paper; store in your freezer for 30 to forty-five minutes or until just frozen.
2. Move the fruit to a food processor. Put in the lime zest and sugar, and pulse until well blended.
3. While the machine runs, add the yogurt and liqueur. Process for another three minutes or until the mixture is fluffy.
4. Pour the mixture into an 8" × 8" pan, cover using foil, and freeze overnight.
5. To serve, let the sherbet temper at room temperature for ten to fifteen minutes, then scoop into glass dishes.

Yield: Servings 4–6

PUMPKIN CUSTARD

Ingredients:

- 1 small cooking pumpkin
- 5 eggs
- 1 cup brown sugar

Directions:

1. With a small sharp knife, cautiously chop the top off of the pumpkin.
2. Using a spoon, remove and discard the seeds and most of the tender flesh; set the pumpkin aside.
3. In a moderate-sized-sized mixing container, whisk the eggs together. Mix in the brown sugar, salt, and coconut cream until well blended.
4. Pour the mixture into the pumpkin.
5. Put the pumpkin in a steamer and allow to steam for roughly twenty minutes or until the custard is set.

Yield: Servings 4

PUMPKIN SIMMERED IN COCONUT MILK

Ingredients:

- ½ cup coconut milk
- ½ teaspoon salt
- 1 cup water
- 2 cups fresh pumpkin meat cut into big julienned pieces (acorn squash is a good substitute)
- 1 cup brown sugar

Directions:

1. Place the water and the coconut milk in a moderate-sized pan using low heat. Put in the salt and half of the sugar; stir until well blended. Adjust the sweetness to your preference by put in more water or sugar if required.
2. Put in the julienned pumpkin to the pan and bring to its boiling point on moderate heat. Reduce to a simmer and cook until soft, approximately 5 to ten minutes depending on both the texture of the pumpkin and your own preference.
3. The pumpkin may be served hot, warm, or cold.

Yield: Servings 4

STEAMED COCONUT CAKES

Ingredients:

- ¼ cup all-purpose flour
- ½ cup coconut milk
- ½ cup grated sweet coconut
- ½ cup rice flour
- 4 tablespoons finely granulated sugar
- 5 eggs
- Pinch of salt

Directions:

1. In a big mixing container, beat the eggs and the sugar together until thick and pale in color.
2. Put in the rice flours and salt.
3. Beating continuously, slowly pour in the coconut milk. Beat the batter for 3 more minutes.
4. Bring some water to boil in a steamer big enough to hold 10 small ramekins. When the water starts to boil, put the ramekins in the steamer to heat for a couple of minutes.
5. Split the shredded coconut uniformly between all of the ramekins and use a spoon to compact it on the bottom of the cups.
6. Pour the batter uniformly between the cups. Steam for about ten minutes.
7. Take away the cakes from the cups the moment they are sufficiently cool to handle.
8. Serve warm or at room temperature.

Yield: 10 cakes

STICKY RICE WITH COCONUT CREAM SAUCE

Ingredients:

- 1 cup coconut cream
- 1 teaspoon salt
- 3 cups cooked Sweet Sticky Rice
- 4 ripe mangoes, thinly cut (or other tropical fruits)
- 4 tablespoons sugar

Directions:

1. For the sauce, put the coconut cream, sugar, and salt in a small deep cooking pan. Stir to blend and bring to its boiling point on moderate to high heat. Decrease the heat and simmer for five minutes.
2. To serve, position mango slices on each plate. Put a mound of rice next to the fruit. Top the rice with some of the sauce.

Yield: Servings 6

SWEET STICKY RICE

Ingredients:

- ½ cup granulated sugar
- ½ teaspoon salt
- 1 cups canned coconut milk
- 1½ cups white glutinous rice

Directions:

1. Put the rice in a container and put in enough water to completely cover the rice. Soak for minimum 4 hours or overnight. Drain.
2. Coat a steamer basket with wet cheesecloth. Spread the rice uniformly over the cheesecloth. Put the container over quickly boiling water. Cover and steam until soft, approximately twenty-five minutes; set aside.
3. In a moderate-sized-sized deep cooking pan, mix the coconut milk, sugar, and salt and heat on moderate to high. Stir until the sugar is thoroughly blended. Pour over the rice, stir until blended, and allow to rest for half an hour
4. To serve, place in small bowls or on plates. Decorate using mangoes, papayas, or other tropical fruit.

Yield: Servings 6

TARO BALLS POACHED IN COCONUT MILK

Ingredients:

- 1 cup brown sugar
- 1 cup cooked taro, mashed
- 1 cup corn flour
- 2 cups glutinous rice flour
- 4 cups coconut milk
- Fresh tropical fruit (not necessary)
- teaspoon salt

Directions:

1. In a big mixing container, mix the rice and the flours.
2. Put in the mashed taro and knead to make a tender dough.
3. Roll into little bite-sized balls and save for later.
4. In a moderate-sized to big deep cooking pan, heat the coconut milk using low heat.
5. Put in the brown sugar and the salt, stirring until blended.
6. Bring the mixture to a low boil and put in the taro balls.
7. Poach the balls for five to ten minutes or until done to your preference.
8. Serve hot in small glass bowls, decorated with tropical fruit.

Yield: Servings 6–12

TOFU WITH SWEET GINGER

Ingredients:

- 1 (2- to 3-inch) piece of ginger, peeled and smashed using the back of a knife
- 1 12-ounce package tender tofu
- 3 cups water
- 1 cup brown sugar

Directions:

1. Put the water, ginger, and brown sugar in a small deep cooking pan. Bring to its boiling point using high heat. Lower the heat to a simmer and allow the sauce to cook for minimum ten minutes. (The longer you allow the mixture to cook, the spicier it will get.)

2. To serve, spoon some of the tofu into dessert bowls and pour some sauce over the top. (This sauce is equally good over plain yogurt.)

Yield: 3 cups of sauce

TROPICAL COCONUT RICE

Ingredients:

- ¼ cup toasted coconut
- 1 cup coconut cream
- 2 cups short-grained rice
- 2 cups water

Directions:

1. Place the rice, water, and coconut cream in a moderate-sized deep cooking pan and mix thoroughly. Bring to its boiling point on moderate to high heat. Decrease the heat and cover with a tight-fitting lid. Cook for fifteen to twenty minutes or until all of the liquid has been absorbed.
2. Allow the rice rest off the heat for five minutes.
3. Fluff the rice and mix in the toasted coconut and fruit.

Yield: Servings 6–8

TROPICAL FRUIT WITH GINGER CREÈME ANGLAISE

Ingredients:

- (1-inch) pieces peeled gingerroot, slightly mashed
- 1 cup half-and-half
- 2 tablespoons sugar A variety of tropical fruits, cut
- 3 egg yolks

Directions:

1. In a small heavy deep cooking pan on moderate to low heat, bring the ginger and the half-and-half to a slight simmer. Do not boil.
2. Meanwhile, whisk together the eggs yolks and the sugar.
3. Slowly pour the hot half-and-half into the egg mixture, stirring continuously so that the eggs do not cook.
4. Pour the custard back into the deep cooking pan and cook on moderate to low heat, stirring continuously using a wooden spoon for five minutes or until slightly thickened.
5. Pour the crèmes anglaise through a mesh strainer into a clean container and let cool completely.
6. Pour over slices of your favorite tropical fruits.

Yield: 1½ cups

WATERMELON ICE

Ingredients:

- ½ cup sugar
- 1 (3-pound) piece of watermelon, rind cut away, seeded, and cut into little chunks (reserve a small amount for decoration if you wish)
- 1 cup water
- 1 tablespoon lime juice
- Mint sprigs (not necessary)

Directions:

1. Put the water and sugar in a small deep cooking pan and bring to its boiling point. Turn off the heat and let cool to room temperature, stirring regularly. Set the pan in a container of ice and continue to stir the syrup until cold.
2. Put the watermelon, syrup, and lime juice in a blender and purée until the desired smoothness is achieved.
3. Pour the purée through a sieve into a 9-inch baking pan. Cover the pan using foil.
4. Put into your freezer the purée for eight hours or until frozen.
5. To serve, scrape the frozen purée with the tines of a fork. Ladle the scrapings into pretty glass goblets and decorate with a small piece of watermelon or mint sprigs.

Yield: Servings 6–8

APPETIZERS

-FLAVOR RICE STICKS

Ingredients:

- 1 pound rice sticks, broken into 3-inch segments
- Cayenne pepper to taste
- Curry powder to taste
- Salt to taste
- Vegetable oil for frying

Directions:

1. Pour 2 to 3 inches of vegetable oil into a big frying pan and heat to 350 degrees. Fry the rice sticks in batches (ensuring not to overcrowd the pan), turning them swiftly as they puff up. After they stop crackling in the oil, move the puffed sticks to paper towels to drain.
2. While the rice sticks are still hot, drizzle salt on 1 batch; drizzle a second batch with curry powder; and a third batch with cayenne pepper to taste.

Yield: Servings 4–6

ASIL AND SHRIMP WEDGES

Ingredients:

- ½ cup julienned basil
- ½ pound cooked salad shrimp
- 1 green onion, trimmed and thinly cut
- 1 teaspoon fish sauce
- 1½ teaspoons vegetable oil, divided
- 2 tablespoons water
- 4 eggs
- Salt and pepper to taste

Directions:

1. Put 1 teaspoon of the vegetable oil in a sauté pan on moderate heat. Put in the shrimp and green onion, and sauté until the shrimp are warmed through, roughly two minutes. Put in the basil and fish sauce and cook for 1 more minute. Set aside.
2. In a big container, whisk together the eggs, water, and salt and pepper, then mix in the shrimp mixture.
3. Put the remaining ½ teaspoon of vegetable oil in an omelet pan on moderate heat. Put in the egg mixture and cook until the omelet starts to brown. Turn over the omelet and carry on cooking until set.
4. To serve, slide the omelet onto a serving plate and cut it into wedges. Serve with a Thai dipping sauce of your choice.

Yield: Servings 4–6 as an appetizer or 2 as a brunch item

CHICKEN, SHRIMP, AND BEEF SATAY

CHICKEN

- 1 recipe Peanut Dipping Sauce
- 1 recipe Thai Marinade
- 3 whole boneless, skinless chicken breasts, cut into lengthy strips about ½-inch wide

Directions:

1. Thread the chicken strips onto presoaked bamboo skewers or onto metal skewers. Put the skewers in a flat pan and cover with marinade. Marinate the chicken in your fridge overnight.
2. Cook the skewers on the grill or under the broiler, coating and turning them until they are thoroughly cooked, approximately six to eight minutes.
3. Serve with the peanut sauce for dipping.

SHRIMP

- 1 recipe Peanut Dipping Sauce
- 1 recipe Thai Marinade

- 24 big shrimp, shelled and deveined

Directions:

1. Thread the shrimp onto presoaked bamboo skewers or onto metal skewers (about 3 shrimp per skewer). Put the skewers in a flat pan and cover with marinade. Marinate the shrimp for minimum fifteen minutes, but no longer than an hour.
2. Cook the skewers on the grill or under the broiler, coating and turning them frequently until just opaque, approximately three to four minutes.
3. Serve with the peanut sauce for dipping.

Yield: 4–6 chicken skewers or 6–8 shrimp or beef skewers

BEEF

- 1 recipe Thai Marinade
- 1 recipe Peanut Dipping Sauce
- 1-1½ pounds sirloin steak, fat and sinew removed, cut into ½-inch-wide strips

Directions:

1. Thread the beef strips onto presoaked bamboo skewers or onto metal skewers. Put the skewers in a flat pan and cover with marinade. Marinate the beef in your fridge overnight.
2. Cook the skewers on the grill or under the broiler, coating and turning them frequently until done to your preference, approximately six to eight minutes for medium.
3. Serve with the peanut sauce for dipping.

CHINESE-STYLE DUMPLINGS

Ingredients:

- ¼ cup sticky rice flour
- ¼ cup tapioca flour
- ½ cup water
- 1 cup rice flour
- 1 tablespoon soy sauce

- 1 teaspoon vegetable oil
- 2 cups chives, cut into ½–inch lengths

Directions:

1. In a moderate-sized-sized deep cooking pan, mix together the sticky rice flour, the rice flour, and the water. Turn the heat to moderate and cook, stirring continuously until the mixture has the consistency of glue. (If the mixture becomes too sticky, decrease the heat to low.) Take away the batter from the heat and swiftly mix in the tapioca flour. Set aside to cool completely.
2. In the meantime, put in the vegetable oil to a frying pan big enough to easily hold the chives, and heat on high. Put in the chives and the soy sauce. Stir-fry the chives just until they wilt. Be careful not to let the chives cook excessively. Turn off the heat and save for later.
3. Once the dough has reached room temperature, check its consistency. If it is too sticky to work with, add a little extra tapioca flour.
4. To make the dumplings, roll the batter into balls an inch in diameter. Using your fingers, flatten each ball into a disk approximately four inches across. Ladle approximately 1 tablespoon of the chives into the middle of each disk. Fold the disk in half and pinch the edges together to make a halfmoon-shaped packet.
5. Put the dumplings in a prepared steamer for five to 8 minutes or until the dough is cooked. Serve with a spicy dipping sauce of your choice.

Yield: 15–20 dumplings

COLD SESAME NOODLES

Ingredients:

- ¼ cup creamy peanut butter or tahini
- ¼–½ teaspoon dried red pepper flakes
- 1 pound angel hair pasta
- 1 tablespoon grated ginger
- 1–2 green onions, trimmed and thinly cut (not necessary)

- 2 tablespoons rice vinegar
- 2 tablespoons sesame oil

Directions:

1. Cook the pasta in accordance with package directions. Wash under cold water, then set aside.
2. Vigorously whisk together the rest of the ingredients; pour over pasta, tossing to coat.
3. Decorate using green onion if you wish.

Yield: Servings 2–4

CRAB SPRING ROLLS

Ingredients:

- ¼–½ teaspoon grated lime peel
- 1 pound crabmeat, picked over to remove any shells, and shredded
- 1 tablespoon mayonnaise
- 2 egg yolks, lightly beaten
- Canola oil for deep frying
- fifteen small, soft Boston lettuce leaves
- fifteen spring roll or egg roll wrappers
- Mint leaves
- Parsley leaves

Directions:

1. In a small container, combine the crabmeat with the mayonnaise and lime peel.
2. Put 1 tablespoon of the crabmeat mixture in the middle of 1 spring roll wrapper. Fold a pointed end of the wrapper over the crabmeat, then fold the opposite point over the top of the folded point. Brush a small amount of the egg yolk over the top of the uncovered wrapper, then fold the bottom point over the crabmeat and roll to make a tight packet; set aside. Repeat with the rest of the crabmeat and wrappers.
3. Heat the oil to 365 degrees in a frying pan or deep fryer. Deep-fry the rolls three to 4 at a time for a couple of minutes or so, until they are a golden brown; drain using paper towels.

4. To serve, wrap each spring roll in a wrapper with a single piece of lettuce, and a drizzling of mint and parsley. Serve with a dipping sauce of your choice.

Yield: fifteen rolls

CRISPY MUSSEL PANCAKES

Ingredients:

- ¼ cup all-purpose flour
- ¼ teaspoon salt
- ½ cup tapioca flour
- ¾ cup water
- 1 cup shelled mussels (approximately 1 pound before shelling)
- 1 teaspoon baking powder
- 2 cups bean sprouts
- 2 tablespoons chopped cilantro, plus extra for decoration
- Salt and ground pepper to taste

Directions:

1. To prepare the mussels, wash them swiftly using cool running water. Debeard the mussels by pulling out the brown membrane that is sometimes still attached. Discard any mussels that are already open. Fill a big frying pan with ½ to an inch of water. Bring the water to its boiling point, then put in the mussels, cover, and allow to steam approximately four minutes or until the mussels have opened, shaking the pan every so frequently. Drain the mussels through a colander. Allow to cool to room temperature and then use a small fork to pull the meat from the shell; set aside using paper towels.
2. In a moderate-sized-sized mixing container, mix together the flours, the salt, and the baking powder. Whisk in the water to make a thin batter.
3. Preheat your oven to 200 degrees. In a large, heavy-bottomed frying pan, heat the vegetable oil on moderate to high heat. Pour half of the batter into the frying pan and top with half of the mussels. Cook until the batter has set and turned golden, approximately 2 minutes. Cautiously flip the pancake over and carry on cooking until golden. Take away the

pancake to a baking sheet lined with some foil and place it in your oven to keep warm. Repeat to make a second pancake with the rest of the batter and mussels.
4. Put in 1 teaspoon of vegetable oil to the frying pan if it is dry, and raise the heat to high. Put in the bean sprouts, drizzle with salt and ground pepper to taste, and stir-fry swiftly just to heat through, approximately half a minute.
5. To serve, place each pancake in the middle of a plate. Top with the bean sprouts, some cilantro, and a grind of fresh pepper. Serve with a sweet-and-sour sauce of your choice.

Yield: Servings 2–4

CURRIED FISH CAKES

Ingredients:

- ¼ cup chopped garlic
- ¼ cup chopped lemongrass, inner portion only
- ¼ cup chopped shallots
- ½ pound French beans, trimmed and finely chopped
- ½ tablespoon salt
- ½ teaspoon peppercorns
- 1 egg, beaten
- 1 pound boneless whitefish steak, minced
- 1 tablespoon chopped ginger
- 1 tablespoon shrimp paste
- 1 teaspoon grated lime peel
- 5–10 dried chilies, seeded, soaked, and shredded
- Vegetable oil for frying

Directions:

1. Put the shallots, garlic, lemongrass, ginger, peppercorns, lime peel, shrimp paste, chilies, and salt in a food processor or blender and process to make a smooth paste.

2. Put in the fish to the food processor and pulse until well blended with the spice paste. Put in the beaten egg and mix one more time. Move the fish mixture to a big mixing container and mix in the green beans.
3. Using roughly 1 tablespoon of fish mixture, form a flat, round cake; repeat until all of the mixture is used.
4. Heat roughly to ¼ inch of vegetable oil to 350 degrees on moderate to high heat in a frying pan or deep fryer; fry the fish cakes until golden.

Serve with a dipping sauce of your choice.

Yield: 15–20 small cakes

FRIED TOFU WITH DIPPING SAUCES

Ingredients:

- 1 package of tofu, cut into bite-sized cubes
- Dipping sauces of your choice
- Vegetable oil for frying

Directions:

1. Put in approximately two to three inches of vegetable oil to a deep fryer or wok. Heat the oil on medium until it reaches about 350 degrees. Cautiously add some of the tofu pieces, ensuring not to overcrowd them; fry until a golden-brown colour is achieved, turning continuously. Move the fried tofu to paper towels to drain as each batch is cooked.
2. Serve the tofu with a choice of dipping sauces, such as Sweet-and-Sour, Peanut, and Mint Dipping Sauce.

Yield: Servings 2–4

FRIED WON TONS

Ingredients:

- ½ cup chopped white mushrooms

- ½ pound ground pork
- 1 clove garlic, minced
- 1 tablespoon soy sauce
- 2 tablespoons minced cilantro
- 25 won ton skins
- Pinch white pepper
- Vegetable oil for frying

Directions:

1. In a moderate-sized-sized mixing container, meticulously mix the garlic, cilantro, soy sauce, mushrooms, white pepper, and ground pork.
2. To make the won tons, place roughly ½ teaspoon of the filling in the center of a won ton skin. Fold the won ton from corner to corner, making a triangle. Push the edges together to secure closed. Repeat with the rest of the skins and filling.
3. Put in approximately two to three inches of vegetable oil to a deep fryer or wok. Heat the oil on medium until it reaches about 350 degrees. Cautiously add the won tons, 2 or 3 at a time. Fry until they become golden brown, turning them continuously. Move the cooked won tons to drain using paper towels as they are done.
4. Serve the won tons with either sweet-and-sour sauce or the sauce of your choice.

Yield: Approximately 25 won tons

MEE KROB

Ingredients:

- ½ cup dried shrimp
- ½ pound thin rice stick noodles, broken into handfuls
- 1 cup bean sprouts
- 1 tablespoon Tamarind Concentrate (Page 29)
- 10 small lime wedges
- 2 eggs, beaten
- 2–3 drops red food coloring

- 5 tablespoons sugar
- 1 cup honey
- 1 cup rice or white vinegar
- Vegetable oil for deep-frying

Directions:

1. Mix the honey, vinegar, sugar, food coloring, and tamarind in a moderate-sized deep cooking pan. Bring the mixture to its boiling point on moderate heat, stirring once in a while. Decrease the heat and simmer for two to three minutes or until the mixture starts to thicken; turn off the heat and save for later.
2. Bring about 3 inches of vegetable oil to 360 degrees in a deep fryer or frying pan. Drop a single layer of the rice stick noodles into the hot oil, ensuring to leave enough room for them to cook uniformly. Turn the noodles using a slotted spoon the moment they start to puff up. Once the noodles are golden, remove them to paper towels to drain. Repeat until all of the noodles are cooked.
3. Put in the dried shrimp to the oil and cook for 45 seconds or so. Remove to paper towels.
4. Pour out all but a thin coat of the oil from the frying pan. Put in the beaten eggs and stir-fry them swiftly, shirring them into lengthy strips. Once they are cooked, remove them to paper towels.
5. Bring the sauce back to its boiling point. Mix in the shrimp and continue to boil for a couple of minutes.
6. Put about of the noodles on a serving platter and spoon about of the sauce over the top; lightly toss to coat the noodles uniformly being cautious not to crush the noodles. Repeat until all of the noodles are coated in sauce.
7. To serve, mound the noodles, put the egg strips over them, and top with the bean sprouts Pass the lime wedges.

Yield: Servings 4–6

OMELET "EGG ROLLS"

Ingredients:

For the filling:

- ½ pound ground pork or chicken
- ½ teaspoon sugar
- 1 cup shredded Chinese cabbage
- 1 tablespoon fish sauce
- 1 tablespoon minced cilantro
- 1 teaspoon vegetable oil
- 2 green onions, trimmed and thinly cut

For the omelets:

- 1 tablespoon soy or fish sauce
- 1 teaspoon vegetable oil
- 6 tablespoons water
- 8 eggs
- Bibb lettuce
- Decorate of your choice
- Soy sauce, fish sauce, and/or hot sauce

Directions:

1. To make the filling: In a moderate-sized-sized frying pan, warm the vegetable oil on moderate heat. Put in the ground meat and sauté until it is no longer pink. Put in the green onions and cabbage and cook until tender. Put in the sugar, fish sauce, and cilantro; cook for 1 more minute. Set the filling aside, keeping it warm.
2. To make the omelets: Mix the eggs, water, and soy sauce in a moderate-sized container. Put an omelet pan on moderate heat for a minute. Put in roughly ¼ teaspoon of vegetable oil, swirling it to coat the pan uniformly. Pour roughly ¼ of the egg mixture into the pan, then allow it to rest for roughly half a minute. When the bottom is firm, flip the omelet and cook until done. Transfer to a plate and cover using foil to keep warm. Repeat to make 3 more omelets.
3. To fill the "Egg Rolls," place 1 omelet in the middle of a plate. Put ¼ of the filling slightly off-center and then roll up. Trim the ends and chop the rolls into bite-sized pieces.
4. To serve, use Bibb lettuce leaves to pick up the rolls. Immerse in additional soy sauce, fish sauce, hot sauce, or other favorite dipping sauce, and put in the decorate of your choice.

Yield: 16–20 pieces

PORK TOAST TRIANGLES

Ingredients:

- ¼ pound of big shrimp, peeled and deveined
- 1 egg
- 1 pound ground pork (the leaner the better)
- 1 tablespoon chopped cilantro
- 1 tablespoon dried shrimp
- 1 tablespoon fish sauce
- 2 cloves garlic, peeled
- 6 slices day-old bread, crusts trimmed off
- Vegetable oil for frying

Directions:

1. Fill a moderate-sized deep cooking pan with water and bring it to its boiling point. Reduce the heat, put in the shrimp, and simmer until the shrimp are opaque. Drain the shrimp and let cool completely. Coarsely cut and save for later.
2. Put the dried shrimp, cilantro, and the garlic in a food processor and pulse until a smooth paste is formed. Put in the reserved shrimp and ground pork; process once more. Put in the egg and fish sauce and process one more time.
3. Spread the mixture uniformly over each slice of bread. Chop the bread into 4 equal slices, either from corner to corner forming triangles or from top to bottom forming squares.
4. Put in roughly ½ inch of vegetable oil to a big frying pan. Bring the oil to roughly 375 degrees on moderate to high heat. Put 4 to 5 toasts in the oil, filling side down. Ensure that the toasts are not crowded in the oil or they will not brown uniformly. After the filling side is well browned, use a slotted spoon or metal strainer to flip the toasts. Watch the toasts cautiously, as the bottoms will brown swiftly. Take away the toasts to a stack of paper towels to drain. Cautiously pat the tops of the toasts using paper towels to remove any oil
5. Serve the toasts with sweet-and-sour or plum sauce.

Yield: 24 pieces

PORK, CARROT, AND CELERY SPRING ROLLS

Ingredients:

- ¼ cup fish sauce
- ¼ teaspoon white pepper
- 1 cup bean sprouts
- 1 cup minced or ground pork
- 1 teaspoon minced garlic
- 2 cups chopped celery
- 2 cups grated carrots
- 2 egg yolks, beaten
- 2 tablespoons sugar
- 2 tablespoons vegetable oil
- 20 spring roll wrappers
- Vegetable oil for deep frying

Directions:

1. In a big frying pan, heat the 2 tablespoons of vegetable oil over moderatehigh heat. Put in the garlic and pork, and sauté until the pork is thoroughly cooked.
2. Put in the carrots, celery, fish sauce, sugar, and white pepper. Increase heat to high and cook for a minute.
3. Drain any liquid from the pan and allow the mixture to cool completely, then mix in the bean sprouts.
4. On a clean, dry work surface, put the egg roll wrapper with an end pointing toward you, making a diamond. Put roughly 2 tablespoons of the filling on the lower portion of the wrapper. Fold up the corner nearest you and roll once, then fold in the sides. Brush the rest of the point with the egg yolk and finish rolling to secure. Repeat with the rest of the wrappers and filling.
5. Heat 2 to 3 inches of oil to 350 degrees. Deep-fry the spring rolls until a golden-brown colour is achieved; remove instantly to drain using paper towels.
6. Serve with sweet-and-sour sauce.

Yield: 20 rolls

RICE PAPER ROLLS

Ingredients:

- 1 cup thin rice noodles
- 4 (8" × 10") sheets of rice paper
- 1 cup grated carrot
- 2 scallions, thinly cut
- 1 small cucumber, shredded 20 mint leaves
- 1 small bunch cilantro
- 8–10 medium to big cooked shrimp, cut in half

Directions:

1. Soak the rice noodles in super hot water until they are soft, usually ten to twenty minutes; drain. You can leave the noodles whole, or cut them into two-inch pieces if you prefer.
2. Put a sanitized kitchen towel on a work surface with a container of hot water nearby. Place a sheet of the rice paper in the hot water for roughly twenty seconds, just until soft; lay it out flat on the towel.
3. In the center of the rice paper, place 2 to 3 pieces of shrimp and ¼ of the noodles, carrots, scallions, and cucumbers. Top with mint and cilantro.
4. Swiftly roll up the rice paper, keeping it quite tight; then roll up the whole thing using plastic wrap, ensuring to keep it tight. Place in your fridge until ready to serve.
5. To serve, trim the ends off the rolls. Chop the remaining roll into pieces and remove the plastic wrap. Serve with a dipping sauce of your choice.

Yield: Servings 2–4

SALT-CURED EGGS

Ingredients:

- 1 dozen eggs
- 1½ cups salt
- 6 cups water

Directions:

1. Mix the water and the salt in a big deep cooking pan and bring to its boiling point using high heat. Turn off the heat and let cool completely.
2. Cautiously place the eggs in a container. Pour the salt water over the eggs and seal the container firmly. Put the container in your fridge and let the eggs cure for minimum 1 month.
3. To serve, hard-boil the eggs, let cool completely, then peel, slice, and enjoy.

Yield: 1 dozen eggs

SHRIMP TOAST

Ingredients:

- ¼ pound ground pork
- ¼ teaspoon salt
- ½ pound shrimp, cleaned, deveined, and crudely chopped
- 1 egg, beaten
- 1 tablespoon chopped cilantro
- 2 cloves garlic, minced
- 2 tablespoons sesame seeds
- 2 teaspoons soy sauce
- 2 teaspoons vegetable oil, divided
- 32 slices cucumber
- 8 slices of white bread, left to sit out overnight, crusts removed
- teaspoon cayenne

Directions:

1. In a small container, mix the shrimp and pork; set aside.
2. In another small container, mix the cilantro, garlic, cayenne, and salt. Pour the spice mixture over the shrimp and pork, and combine.
3. Mix in the beaten egg and soy sauce; mix thoroughly. Split the mixture into 8 parts.

4. Smoothly spread a slim layer of the mixture on each slice of bread and drizzle with sesame seeds.
5. Heat ¼ teaspoon vegetable oil in nonstick frying pan. When it is super hot, place 1 piece of bread, meat side down, in the oil. Cook until golden in color, then remove to a paper towel, blotting any surplus oil. Repeat for all of the bread sides.
6. Cut each slice of bread into four equivalent portions and top each quarter with a cucumber slice.

Yield: 32 pieces

SKEWERED THAI PORK

Ingredients:

- 1 pound pork, thinly cut into lengthy strips
- 1 tablespoon coconut milk
- 1 tablespoon fish sauce
- 1 teaspoon salt
- 2 tablespoons sugar
- 20–30 bamboo skewers, soaked in water for an hour
- 3 cloves garlic, minced

Directions:

1. In a moderate-sized-sized container, mix the sugar, salt, garlic, fish sauce, and coconut milk.
2. Toss the pork strips in the mixture to coat completely. Cover the container and marinate for minimum 30 minutes, but if possible overnight in your fridge.
3. Thread the pork strips onto the bamboo skewers.
4. Grill the skewers for approximately 3 to five minutes per side.
5. Serve with your favorite sauce or as is.

Yield: Servings 2–3

SON-IN-LAW EGGS

Ingredients:

- ¼ cup chopped cilantro
- ¼ cup vegetable oil
- 10 hard-boiled eggs, cooled and peeled
- 2 shallots, thinly cut
- 3 tablespoons fish sauce
- 1 cup light brown sugar
- 1 cup Tamarind Concentrate (Page 29)
- Dried hot chili flakes to taste

Directions:

1. Heat the vegetable oil in a frying pan on moderate heat. Put the whole eggs in the frying pan and fry until a golden-brown colour is achieved. Take away the eggs to paper towels and save for later. (If your frying pan can't hold all of the eggs easily, do this in batches.)
2. Put in the shallots to the frying pan and sauté until just starting to brown. Take away the shallots from the oil using a slotted spoon and save for later.
3. Place the brown sugar, fish sauce, and tamarind in the frying pan. Stir to blend and bring to a simmer. Cook the mixture, stirring continuously, until the sauce thickens, approximately five minutes; turn off the heat.
4. Chop the eggs in half vertically and put them face-up on a rimmed serving dish. Spread the shallots over the eggs and then sprinkle the eggs with the sauce. Decorate using cilantro and chili pepper flakes.

Yield: 20

SPICY COCONUT BUNDLES

Ingredients:

- ½ cup chopped lime segments
- ½ cup chopped peanuts

- ½ cup diced red onion
- ½ cup dried shrimp
- 1 cup shredded fresh coconut
- 1–2 jalapeños, seeded and cut
- 20–25 moderate-sized spinach leaves, washed and patted dry
- 1 cup brown sugar
- 1 cup shrimp paste

Directions:

1. Put the coconut in a moderate-sized sauté pan and cook on moderate heat until browned, approximately twenty minutes; allow to cool.
2. In a small deep cooking pan, melt the brown sugar on moderate heat, stirring continuously. Stir in the shrimp paste until well blended. Set the sauce aside.
3. Put the coconut, onion, lime pieces, peanuts, dried shrimp, and jalapeños in a moderate-sized serving container; lightly toss to blend.
4. To serve, place four to 5 spinach leaves (depending on the size of the leaves) on each serving plate. Top each leaf with roughly 1 tablespoon of the coconut mixture and sprinkle a small amount of sauce over the coconut.
5. To eat, roll up the spinach leaf around the coconut mixture and pop the whole bundle in your mouth. Pass additional sauce separately.

Yield: Servings 4

SPICY GROUND PORK IN BASIL LEAVES

Ingredients:

- ¼ tablespoon (or to taste) ground dried chili pepper
- ½ pound ground pork
- 1 shallot, thinly cut
- 1 tablespoon toasted rice powder (available in Asian specialty stores)
- 3 tablespoons fish sauce
- 5 sprigs cilantro, chopped

- Juice of 1–2 limes
- Lettuce and/or big basil leaves

Directions:

1. Squeeze the juice of half of a lime over the ground pork and let marinate for a few minutes.
2. Heat a big frying pan on high. Put in a couple of tablespoons of water and then instantly put in the pork; stir-fry until the pork is thoroughly cooked. (It is okay if the pork sticks at first — it will ultimately loosen.)
3. Pour off any fat that has collected in the pan and then put the pork in a big mixing container. Put in the remaining lime juice (to taste), fish sauce, shallot, ground chili pepper, cilantro, and toasted rice; stir until blended meticulously.
4. To serve, put the mixture in a serving container and let guests use the lettuce and basil leaves to scoop out the mixture.

Yield: Servings 4

SPICY SCALLOPS

Ingredients:

- 1 (½-inch) piece of ginger, peeled and minced
- 1 clove garlic, minced
- 1 jalapeño, seeded and minced
- 1 teaspoon vegetable oil
- 2 tablespoons soy sauce
- 2 tablespoons water
- 8 big scallops, cleaned
- teaspoon ground coriander

Directions:

1. In a pan big enough to hold all of the scallops, heat the oil on moderate heat. Put in the garlic, jalapeño, and ginger, and stir-fry for approximately one minute.

2. Put in the coriander, soy sauce, and water, stirring to blend; simmer for two to three minutes. Strain the liquid through a fine-mesh sieve. Allow the pan to cool slightly.
3. Put in the scallops to the pan and spoon the reserved liquid over the top of them. Return the pan to the stove, increasing the heat to moderate-high. Cover the pan and let the scallops steam for approximately two to three minutes, or until done to your preference. Serve instantly.

Yield: Servings 4

THAI FRIES

Ingredients:

- 1 14-ounce bag shredded sweetened coconut
- 1 cup rice flour
- 1 cup sticky rice flour
- 1 pound taro root
- 1 teaspoon black pepper
- 1 teaspoon salt
- 2 moderate-sized sweet potatoes
- 2 tablespoons sugar
- 3 tablespoons black sesame seeds
- 4 green plantains
- Water

Directions:

1. Peel the root vegetables and cut them into flat -inch-thick strips about 3 inches long and a inch wide.
2. Mix the flours in a big mixing container and mix in ½ cup of water. Continue putting in water ¼ cup at a time until a mixture resembling pancake batter is formed. Mix in rest of the ingredients.
3. Fill a moderate-sized deep cooking pan a third to a half full with vegetable oil. Heat the oil using high heat until super hot, but not smoking.

4. Put in some of the vegetables to the batter, coating them thoroughly. Using a slotted spoon or Asian strainer, put the vegetables in the hot oil. (Be careful here: The oil may spatter.) Fry the vegetables, turning them once in a while, until a golden-brown colour is achieved. Move the fried vegetables to a stack of paper towels to drain, then serve instantly.

Yield: Servings 4–8

SOUPS

ASIAN CHICKEN NOODLE SOUP

Ingredients:

- ½ cup chopped onion
- 1 carrot, peeled and julienned
- 1 cup chopped cilantro
- 1 moderate-sized sweet red pepper, seeded and julienned
- 2 cups chicken broth
- 2 star anise
- 2 tablespoons chopped ginger
- 2 tablespoons fish sauce
- 2 tablespoons vegetable oil
- 2 whole boneless, skinless chicken breasts, cut into lengthy strips
- 3 cloves garlic, minced
- 3 ounces snow peas, trimmed
- 4 ounces, cellophane noodles, soaked in boiling water for five minutes and drained
- 5 cups water, divided
- Lemon or lime wedges
- Peanuts, crudely chopped

Directions:

1. In a big deep cooking pan, heat the oil on high. Put in the onion and sauté until translucent. Put in the ginger, garlic, and cilantro, and sauté for 1 more minute. Mix in the broth and 2 cups of the water. Put in the star anise. Bring to its boiling point, reduce heat, and cover; simmer for twenty minutes to half an hour.
2. In another deep cooking pan, bring the rest of the water to its boiling point. Put in the vegetables and blanch for a minute or until soft-crisp. Drain and run very cold water over the vegetables to stop the cooking process; set aside.

3. Strain the broth into a clean soup pot and bring to its boiling point. Put in the chicken strips and reduce heat. Poach the chicken using low heat until opaque, roughly ten minutes. Put in the cellophane noodles and reserved vegetables, and carry on simmering for two more minutes. Season to taste with fish sauce.
4. To serve, ladle the soup into warm bowls. Drizzle with peanuts and decorate with lime wedge.

Yield: Servings 4 to 6

CHICKEN SOUP WITH LEMONGRASS

Ingredients:

- ¾ pound boneless, skinless chicken breast, trimmed and slice into bite-sized pieces
- 1 (14-ounce) can unsweetened coconut milk
- 1 (1-inch) piece ginger, cut into 6 pieces
- 1 clove garlic, minced
- 1 medium onion, minced
- 1 stalk lemongrass, trimmed, bruised, and slice into 2 to 3 pieces
- 1 tablespoon vegetable oil
- 2 cups wild or domestic mushrooms, cut into bite-sized pieces (if required)
- 2 tablespoons fish sauce
- 2 teaspoons prepared Red Curry Paste or curry powder
- 3 lime leaves (fresh or dried)
- 4 cups chicken broth
- Juice of 2 limes
- Salt and pepper to taste

Directions:

1. In a moderate-sized-sized deep cooking pan, mix the oil, onion, and garlic. Cook on moderate heat for a minute. Put in the lemongrass, curry paste, ginger, and lime leaves.
2. Cook while stirring, for about three minutes, then put in the broth. Bring to its boiling point, decrease the heat to moderate, and carry on cooking for ten more minutes.

3. Put in the coconut milk, the chicken pieces, and the mushrooms. Continue to cook for five minutes or until the chicken is done.
4. Mix in the lime juice and fish sauce. Sprinkle salt and pepper to taste.
5. Take away the lemongrass, lime leaves, and ginger pieces before you serve.

Yield: Servings 4–6

CHILLED MANGO SOUP

Ingredients:

- 1 cup plain yogurt
- 1 tablespoon dry sherry
- 1 teaspoon sugar (not necessary)
- 1½ cups chilled chicken or vegetable broth
- 2 big mangoes, peeled, pitted, and chopped
- Salt and white pepper to taste

Directions:

1. Put all of the ingredients in a blender or food processor and process until the desired smoothness is achieved. Adjust seasonings.
2. This soup may be served instantly or placed in the fridge until needed. If you do place in your fridge the soup, allow it to sit at room temperature for about ten minutes or so before you serve to take some of the chill off.

Yield: Servings 2–4

LEMONY CHICKEN SOUP

Ingredients:

- ½ cup lemon slices, including peel
- 1 cup straw mushrooms
- 1 tablespoon minced fresh ginger
- 1 whole boneless, skinless chicken breast, poached and shredded

- 1½ cups coconut milk
- 1½ teaspoons fresh hot chili pepper, seeded and chopped
- 1½ teaspoons sugar
- 2 cups chicken broth
- 2 green onions, thinly cut
- 3 tablespoons fish sauce
- 3 teaspoons lemongrass, peeled and chopped

Directions:

1. Mix the lemon slices, fish sauce, chili pepper, green onion, and sugar in a small glass container; set aside.
2. Mix the coconut milk, chicken broth, lemongrass, mushrooms, and ginger in a deep cooking pan. Bring to its boiling point, reduce heat, and simmer for twenty to twenty-five minutes. Put in the chicken and lemon mixture; heat through.
3. To serve, ladle into warmed bowls.

Yield: Servings 4–6

PUMPKIN SOUP

Ingredients:

For the broth:

- 1 clove of garlic, halved
- 1 moderate-sized leek, cut
- 1 red chili pepper, cut in half and seeded
- 1 small banana, cut
- 1 small pumpkin, peeled, seeded, and cut into little chunks
- 1 tablespoon finely chopped ginger
- 1 tablespoon Green Curry Paste
- 1½ stalks celery, cut
- 2 tablespoons butter
- 3 stalks lemongrass, peeled and thinly cut

- 3¼ cups vegetable broth
- 1 cup coconut milk
- 1 cup half-and-half
- Salt and pepper to taste

For the chicken and vegetables:

- ¾ cup cooked rice
- 1 small Japanese eggplant, cut into 4 pieces
- 1 tablespoon vegetable oil
- 1 whole boneless, skinless chicken breast, trimmed and slice into strips
- 2 kaffir lime leaves, cut into strips
- 2 red chili peppers, cut in half and seeded (not necessary)
- 2 tablespoons butter
- 2 teaspoons finely chopped ginger
- 2 teaspoons prepared Green Curry Paste
- Thai basil

Yield: Servings 4

Directions:

1. In a big pot, melt the butter on moderate heat. Put in the pumpkin, leeks, celery, bananas chili pepper, lemongrass, garlic, and ginger; sweat for five minutes.
2. In another sauté pan, heat the vegetable oil. Put in the eggplant and sauté until just warmed through.
3. Melt the butter in a heavy-bottomed sauté pan on moderate heat. Put in the chicken strips, ginger, lime leaves, and curry paste. Sauté until the chicken is cooked, but not browned. Put in the chicken mixture to the broth.
4. Put in the half-and-half, coconut milk, and curry paste; simmer for fifteen to twenty minutes.
5. Put in the vegetable broth and heat until warm.
6. Take away the chili pepper halves. Move the broth mixture to a blender or food processor and purée until the desired smoothness is achieved. Strain if you wish, and season to taste

with salt and pepper. Pour the mixture into a clean pot and keep warm. To prepare the chicken and vegetables:
7. To prepare the broth:
8. To serve, split the rice among 4 soup bowls. Ladle the broth over the rice. Top with a piece of eggplant, a chili pepper half (if you wish), and some basil.

SPICY SEAFOOD SOUP

Ingredients:

- ¼ cup cut green onions
- 1 pound moderate-sized raw shrimp, peeled and deveined, shells reserved
- 1 quart water
- 1 tablespoon vegetable oil
- 10 (-inch-thick) slices fresh ginger
- 2 fresh serrano chilies, seeded and chopped
- 2 quarts fish or chicken stock
- 2 tablespoons fish sauce
- 2 tablespoons lime juice
- 24 fresh mussels, cleaned
- 3 stalks lemongrass, peeled and chopped
- 3 tablespoons chopped fresh cilantro
- 6–8 kaffir lime leaves
- Red pepper flakes to taste
- Salt
- Zest of 1 lime, grated

Directions:

1. Heat the vegetable oil in a big deep cooking pan. Put in the shrimp shells and sauté until they turn bright pink. Put in the stock, water, lemongrass, lime zest, lime leaves, ginger, and serrano chilies. Bring to its boiling point, reduce heat, and simmer for half an hour Strain the broth into a clean soup pot.

2. Bring the broth to its boiling point. Put in the mussels, cover, and cook until the shells open, approximately 2 minutes. Use a slotted spoon to remove the mussels, discarding any that have not opened. Take away the top shell of each mussel and discard. Set aside the mussels on the half shell.
3. Put in the shrimp to the boiling broth and cook until they are opaque, approximately 2 minutes. Decrease the heat to low.
4. Put in the mussels to the pot. Mix in the lime juice, fish sauce, cilantro, red pepper flakes, and green onions. Simmer for one to two minutes. Season to taste with salt.
5. Serve instantly.

Yield: Servings 4–6

THAI-SPICED BEEF SOUP WITH RICE NOODLES

Ingredients:

- ¼ cup fish sauce
- ¾ cup leftover beef roast, chopped or shredded
- 1 (2–inch) cinnamon stick
- 1 stalk lemongrass, tough outer leaves removed, inner core crushed and minced
- 1 tablespoon prepared chiligarlic sauce
- 1 whole star anise, crushed
- 2 (¼–inch) pieces peeled gingerroot
- 2½ tablespoons lime juice
- 3–4 teaspoons (or to taste) salt
- 8 cups beef broth
- 8 ounces rice noodles, soaked in hot water for approximately ten minutes, strained and washed in cold water
- Freshly ground black pepper to taste

Directions:

1. In a moderate-sized-sized deep cooking pan, simmer the beef broth, star anise, cinnamon stick, and ginger using low heat for thirty to forty minutes.
2. Strain the stock and return to the deep cooking pan.

3. Put in the noodles, lemongrass, shredded beef, fish sauce, chili sauce, and garlic. Bring the soup to its boiling point on moderate heat. Decrease the heat and simmer for five minutes. Mix in the lime juice, salt, and pepper.

Yield: Servings 4–6

TOM KA KAI

Ingredients:

- 1 (1-inch) piece ginger, cut thinly
- 1 (2-inch) piece of lemongrass, bruised
- 1 boneless, skinless chicken breast, cut into bite-sized pieces
- 1 teaspoon cut kaffir lime leaves
- 2 cups chicken broth
- 2 tablespoons lime juice
- 2–4 Thai chilies (to taste), slightly crushed
- 4 tablespoons fish sauce
- 5 ounces coconut milk

Directions:

1. In a moderate-sized-sized soup pot, heat the broth on medium. Put in the lime leaves, lemongrass, ginger, fish sauce, and lime juice.
2. Bring the mixture to its boiling point, put in the chicken and coconut milk, and bring to its boiling point once more.
3. Reduce the heat, put in the chilies, and cover; allow to simmer until the chicken is thoroughly cooked, approximately 3 to five minutes.
4. Take away the chilies and the lemongrass stalk using a slotted spoon before you serve.

Yield: Servings 4–6

TOM YUM

Ingredients:

- 1 can straw mushrooms, drained
- 2 stalks lemongrass, bruised and slice into 1-inch-long segments
- 2 tablespoons fish sauce
- 2 tablespoons minced fresh ginger
- 20 moderate-sized shrimp, shelled but with tails left on
- 2–3 teaspoons cut kaffir lime leaves or lime zest
- 2–3 Thai chili peppers, seeded and minced
- 3 shallots, finely chopped
- 3 tablespoons lime juice
- 4–5 cups water

Directions:

1. Pour the water into a moderate-sized soup pot. Put in the shallots, lemongrass, fish sauce and ginger. Bring to its boiling point, reduce heat, and simmer for about three minutes.
2. Put in the shrimp and mushrooms, and cook until the shrimp turn pink. Mix in the lime zest, lime juice, and chili peppers.
3. Cover and take out of the heat. Allow the soup to steep for five to ten minutes before you serve.

Yield: Servings 4–6

VEGETARIAN LEMONGRASS SOUP

Ingredients:

- ½ cup crudely shredded carrots
- ½ cup cut celery
- 1 can straw mushrooms, drained
- 1 cup snow peas, trimmed
- 1 red serrano chili, seeded and thinly cut
- 1 teaspoon (or to taste) crushed red peppers
- 4 tablespoons soy sauce
- 4–6 stalks lemongrass, bruised

- 8 cups low-sodium vegetable broth
- Juice of ½ lime or to taste

Directions:

1. Bring the broth to a simmer in a big deep cooking pan. Put in the crushed red peppers, lemongrass, soy sauce, and lime juice. Simmer for about ten minutes.
2. Put in the rest of the ingredients. Continue to simmer until the vegetables are just done, approximately two to three minutes. Take away the lemongrass stalks before you serve.

Yield: Servings 4–6

SALADS

ASIAN NOODLE AND VEGETABLE SALAD

Ingredients:

- ¼ pound snow peas, trimmed and cut on the diagonal
- ½ cup toasted peanuts, chopped
- 1 cup bean sprouts
- 1 lime, cut into 6–8 wedges
- 1 medium carrot, peeled and thinly cut on the diagonal
- 1 recipe Spicy Thai Dressing (see recipe on page 28)
- 1 small red bell pepper, cored, seeded, and slice into fine strips
- 1 teaspoon sesame oil
- 1 teaspoon soy sauce
- 10 basil leaves, shredded (if possible Thai or lemon)
- 2 teaspoons vegetable oil
- 4 green onions, thinly cut
- 8 ounces dried rice noodles, cooked firm to the bite and washed under cold water

Directions:

1. In a big container, toss the noodles with the oils and the soy sauce.
2. Blanch the snow peas in boiling water for half a minute and then wash them under cold water.
3. Put in the snow peas, bell pepper, and the carrot to the noodles and toss.
4. Sprinkle the Spicy Thai Dressing over the noodle mixture to taste, put in the basil, half of the green onions, and half of the bean sprouts, and toss thoroughly.
5. To serve, put the noodle salad on a chilled serving platter. Spread the rest of the green onions, remaining bean sprouts, and the peanuts over the top. Squeeze the juice of 2 lime wedges over the whole dish, and use the rest of the wedges as decorate. Serve instantly.

Yield: Servings 4–6

CRUNCHY COCONUT-FLAVORED SALAD

Ingredients:

- 1 cup julienned jicama
- 1 medium cucumber, peeled, seeded, and julienned
- 1 recipe Coconut Marinade (Page 21)
- 2–3 tablespoons chopped fresh basil

Directions:

1. Put the jicama, cucumber, and basil in a big container.
2. Pour the marinade over the vegetables and allow to rest in your fridge for minimum 2 hours before you serve.

Yield: Servings 2–3

CUCUMBER SALAD WITH LEMONGRASS

Ingredients:

- ¼ cup minced mint
- ¼ cup minced parsley
- ½ cup shredded carrot
- ½ cup white vinegar
- 1 cup bean sprouts
- 1 cup cubed tart apple (such as Granny Smith)
- 1 garlic clove, very thoroughly minced
- 1 tablespoon fish sauce
- 1 tablespoon vegetable oil
- 1 Thai chili, very thoroughly minced
- 2 stalks lemongrass
- 3 cups thinly cut cucumber

Directions:

1. In a small deep cooking pan, mix the vinegar, chili, and garlic. Bring the mixture to its boiling point. Cover the pan, take it off the heat, and allow to cool.
2. Trim and finely cut 1 lemongrass stalk. Put it in a small deep cooking pan with ½ cup of water, cover, and bring to its boiling point. Turn off heat and allow to cool.
3. Trim the rest of the lemongrass stalk, peel off the tough outer layers, and finely mince the white portion of the soft stalk within. Reserve roughly 1 tablespoon.
4. Mix the cucumber, bean sprouts, apple, carrot, mint, and parsley in a big mixing container In a small container mix the fish sauce, oil, minced lemongrass, the vinegar mixture, and the lemongrass water.
5. Toss the vegetables with the lemongrass vinaigrette to taste.

Yield: Servings 6–8

FIERY BEEF SALAD

Ingredients:

For the dressing:

- ¼ cup basil leaves
- ¼ cup lemon juice
- ¼ teaspoon black pepper
- 2 cloves garlic
- 2 tablespoons brown sugar
- 2 tablespoons chopped serrano chilies
- 2 tablespoons fish sauce

For the salad:

- ½ cup mint leaves
- 1 pound beef steak
- 1 small cucumber, finely cut
- 1 small red onion, finely cut
- 1 stalk lemongrass, outer leaves removed and discarded, inner stalk finely cut
- 1 tomato, finely cut

- Bibb or romaine lettuce leaves
- Salt and pepper to taste

Directions:

1. Mix all of the dressing ingredients in a blender and pulse until well blended; set aside.
2. Flavour the steak with salt and pepper. Over a hot fire, grill to moderate-rare (or to your preference). Move the steak to a platter, cover using foil, and allow to rest for five to ten minutes before carving.
3. Cut the beef across the grain into thin slices.
4. Put the beef slices, any juices from the platter, and the rest of the salad ingredients, apart from the lettuce, in a big mixing container. Put in the dressing and toss to coat.
5. To serve, place lettuce leaves on separate plates and mound the beef mixture on top of the lettuce.

Yield: Servings 2–4

GRILLED CALAMARI SALAD

Ingredients:

For the dressing:

- 1 small onion, thinly cut
- 1 stalk lemongrass, inner core finely chopped
- 1 tablespoon fish sauce
- 1–5 red chili peppers, seeded and chopped
- 3 kaffir lime leaves, chopped or 1 tablespoon lime zest
- 5 teaspoons lime juice
- 1 cup water

For the salad:

- 1 green onion, thinly cut
- 1 pound calamari, cleaned
- 6–8 sprigs cilantro, chopped

- Baby greens (not necessary)
- fifteen–20 mint leaves, chopped

Directions:

1. Mix all the dressing ingredients in a small container; set aside.
2. Prepare a grill or broiler. Put the calamari on a broiler pan or in a grill basket and cook using high heat until soft, approximately 3 minutes per side. Allow to cool to room temperature.
3. Put the grilled calamari in a mixing container. Mix the dressing and pour it over the calamari.
4. If serving instantly, put in the mint, cilantro, and green onions. If you don't like this method, allow the calamari to marinate for maximum 1 hour before you serve, and then put in the additional ingredients.
5. To serve: Use individual cups or bowls to help capture some of the wonderful dressing. If you don't like this method, mound the calamari mixture over a bed of baby greens and spoon additional dressing over the top.

Yield: Servings 2–4

PAPAYA SALAD

Ingredients:

- ½ cup long beans (green beans), cut into 1–inch pieces
- ½–1 teaspoon salt
- 1 medium papaya, peeled and julienned, or cut into little pieces
- 2 teaspoons fish sauce
- 2 tomatoes, thinly cut
- 3 jalapeño peppers, seeded and thinly cut
- 4 tablespoons Tamarind Concentrate (Page 29)
- 4–6 cloves of garlic, chopped crudely
- Sticky rice, cooked in accordance with package directions

Directions:

1. Put the papaya on a sheet pan and drizzle it with salt. Allow the papaya stand for half an hour Pour off any juice and then squeeze the fruit with your hands to extract as much fluid as you can. Put the pulp of the papaya in a big food processor.
2. Put in the chilies and pulse for a short period of time to blend. Put in the rest of the ingredients except the tomato and pulse again until combined.
3. Move the papaya mixture to a serving container and decorate with tomato slices. Serve with sticky rice.

Yield: Servings 4–6

SHRIMP AND NOODLE SALAD

Ingredients:

- ½–1 teaspoon dried red pepper flakes
- ¾ cup lime juice (roughly 4–5 limes)
- 1 clove garlic, minced
- 1 cup citrus fruit (oranges, grapefruit, tangerines, etc.) peeled, sectioned, and chopped
- 1 medium tomato, peeled, seeded, and chopped
- 1 stalk lemongrass, thoroughly minced (inner core only)
- 1 tablespoon brown sugar
- 1 tablespoon vegetable oil
- 2 tablespoons fish sauce
- 24 medium shrimp, peeled and deveined
- 3 green onions, cut
- 8 ounces rice noodles
- 1 cup chopped cilantro, plus extra for decoration
- 1 cup chopped mint leaves
- 1 cup chopped peanuts, plus extra for decoration
- Salt and ground pepper to taste

Directions:

1. Soak the rice noodles in hot water for ten to twenty minutes or until tender. While the noodles are soaking, bring a big pot of water to boil.

2. In the meantime, in a big container, combine the lemongrass, citrus, peanuts, tomato, scallions, mint, and cilantro.
3. In a small container, mix the red pepper flakes, garlic, sugar, lime juice, and fish sauce. (Adjust seasoning to your taste.)
4. Drain the noodles from their soaking liquid and put in them to the boiling water. When the water returns to its boiling point, drain them again and wash meticulously with cold water. Allow the noodles to drain well.
5. Put in the noodles and the dressing to the citrus mixture and toss to blend. Set aside.
6. Brush the shrimp with the vegetable oil and sprinkle with salt and pepper. Grill or sauté for roughly two minutes per side or until done to your preference.
7. To serve, mound the noodles in the middle of a serving platter. Put the grilled shrimp on top and decorate with peanuts and cilantro.

Yield: Servings 6

SPICY RICE SALAD

Ingredients:

For the dressing:

- ¼ cup hot chili oil
- ¼ cup lime juice
- ¼ cup sesame oil
- ½ cup fish sauce
- ½ cup rice vinegar

For the salad:

- 2 cups long-grained rice (if possible Jasmine)
- 2 carrots, peeled and diced
- 1 sweet red pepper, seeded and diced
- 1 serrano chili pepper, seeded and minced
- ¼–½ cup chopped mint
- ¼–½ cup chopped cilantro

- 1 pound cooked shrimp
- 1 cup chopped unsalted peanuts
- Lime wedges
- 4–6 green onions, trimmed and thinly cut

Directions:

1. Whisk together all of the dressing ingredients; set aside.
2. Cook the rice in accordance with the package directions. Fluff the rice, then move it to a big mixing container. Allow the rice to cool slightly.
3. Pour roughly of the dressing over the rice and fluff to coat. Continue to fluff the rice every so frequently until it is completely cooled.
4. Put in the green onions, carrots, red pepper, serrano chili pepper, mint, cilantro, and shrimp to the rice. Toss with the rest of the dressing to taste.
5. To serve, place on separate plates and decorate with peanuts and lime wedges.

Yield: Approximately 8 cups

SPICY SHRIMP SALAD

Ingredients:

For the dressing:

- 2 tablespoons prepared chili sauce
- 3 tablespoons sugar
- 4 tablespoons fish sauce
- 1 cup lime juice

For the salad:

- ¼ cup chopped mint
- ¾ pound cooked shrimp
- 1 small red onion, thinly cut
- 2 cucumbers, peeled and thinly cut
- 2 green onions, trimmed and thinly cut

- Bibb lettuce leaves

Directions:

1. In a small container, mix all the dressing ingredients. Stir until the sugar dissolves completely.
2. In a big container, mix all of the salad ingredients apart from the lettuce. Pour the dressing over and toss to coat.
3. To serve, put the lettuce leaves on separate plates. Mound a portion of the shrimp salad on top of the leaves. Serve instantly.

Yield: Servings 2–4

SWEET-AND-SOUR CUCUMBER SALAD

Ingredients:

- ½ cup rice or white vinegar
- 1 cup boiling water
- 1 small red onion, cut
- 1 teaspoon salt
- 2 medium cucumbers, seeded and cut
- 2 Thai chilies, seeded and minced
- 5 tablespoons sugar

Directions:

1. In a small container, mix the sugar, salt, and boiling water. Stir to meticulously dissolve sugar and salt. Put in the vinegar and allow the vinaigrette to cool completely.
2. Put the cucumbers, onion slices, and the chili peppers in a medium-sized container. Pour the dressing over the vegetables. Cover and let marinate in your fridge minimum until col if possible overnight.

Yield: Servings 2–4

THAI DINNER SALAD

Ingredients:

For the dressing:

- ¾ teaspoon rice wine vinegar
- 1 clove garlic, minced
- 1 tablespoon lemon juice
- 1 tablespoon water
- 2 tablespoons fish sauce
- 2 teaspoons sugar
- Pinch of red pepper flakes

For the salad:

- ¼ cup chopped cilantro
- ¼ cup chopped mint leaves
- 1 cucumber, peeled, seeded, and diced
- 1 small head of romaine or Bibb lettuce, torn into bitesized pieces
- 2 small carrots, grated
- Chopped unsalted peanuts (not necessary)

Directions:

1. In a small container, mix together all of the salad dressing ingredients; set aside.
2. In a big container, toss together all of the salad ingredients. Put in dressing to taste and toss until thoroughly coated. Drizzle chopped peanuts over the top of each salad, if you wish.

Yield: Servings 2–4

THAILAND BAMBOO SHOOTS

Ingredients:

- 1 20-ounce can of bamboo shoots, shredded, liquid reserved

- 1 teaspoon fish sauce
- 1 teaspoon ground dried chili pepper
- 2 green onions, cut
- 2 tablespoons finely crushed peanuts, divided
- Juice of ½ lime
- Sticky rice, cooked in accordance with package directions

Directions:

1. Put the shredded bamboo shoots and roughly ¼ cup (half) of the reserved bamboo liquid in a moderate-sized deep cooking pan. Bring the contents of the pan to its boiling point, reduce heat, and allow to simmer until soft, approximately five minutes. Turn off the heat.
2. Mix in the lime juice, chili pepper, green onions, fish sauce, and 1 tablespoon of the peanuts.
3. Serve with sticky rice, sprinkled with the rest of the peanuts.

Yield: Servings 4

THAILAND SEAFOOD SALAD

Ingredients:

- ¼ cup fish sauce
- ½ pound salad shrimp
- ½ pound squid rings, poached in salted water for half a minute
- 1 (6-ounce) can chopped clams, drained
- 1 clove garlic, minced
- 1 green onion, trimmed and thinly cut
- 1 small onion, finely chopped
- 1 small serrano chili, seeded and finely chopped
- 1 stalk celery, cleaned and thinly cut
- 1 stalk lemongrass, outer leaves removed, inner core minced
- 2 medium cucumbers, peeled, halved, seeded, and super slimly cut
- 2 tablespoons chopped mint
- Bibb lettuce leaves

- Sugar to taste

Directions:

1. In a big mixing container, gently mix the squid, shrimp, clams, cucumber, and celery; set aside.
2. In a small mixing container, mix together the onion, lemongrass, serrano chili, mint, garlic, green onion, and fish sauce. Put in sugar to taste.
3. Pour the dressing over the seafood mixture, tossing to coat. Cover and allow it to sit for minimum 30 minutes before you serve.
4. To serve, place lettuce leaves in the middle of four to 6 plates. Mound the seafood salad on top of the lettuce leaves.

Yield: Servings 4–6

ZESTY MELON SALAD

Ingredients:

- ¼ cup honey
- ¼ teaspoon salt
- 1 serrano chili, seeded and minced (for a hotter salad, leave the seeds in)
- 2 cucumbers, peeled, halved, seeded, and cut
- 6 cups assorted melon cubes
- 6–8 tablespoons lime juice
- Zest of 1 lime

Directions:

1. In a big mixing container, mix the melon and the cucumber.
2. Combine the rest of the ingredients together in a small container. Pour over the fruit and toss thoroughly to coat.
3. Serve instantly, or if you prefer a zestier flavor, let the salad sit for maximum 2 hours to allow the chili flavor to develop.

Yield: Servings 4–6

ABOUT THE AUTHOR

Born and brought up in Thailand, Urassaya Manaying is a professional cook and nutritionist who specializes in traditional Thai recipes. She is best known for her cookbooks on Thai Cooking.

Printed in Great Britain
by Amazon